Over 65 easy cards

explore

creating cards

with Scrapbook Embellishments

MARYJO MCGRAW

North Light Books
Cincinnati, Ohio
www.artistsnetwork.com

09 08 07 06 05   5 4 3 2 1

Library of Congress Cataloging-in-Publication Data

McGraw, MaryJo
    Creating cards with scrapbook embellishments / MaryJo McGraw.
         p. cm.
    Includes index.
    ISBN 1-58180-628-0
    1. Greeting cards. I. Title.

TT872.M3335 2005
745.594--dc22

20044057574

Editor: Krista Hamilton
Designer: Leigh Ann Lentz
Layout Artist: Jessica Schultz
Production Coordinator: Robin Richie
Photographer: Christine Polomsky and Tim Grondin
Photography Stylist: Nora Martini

F+W PUBLICATIONS, INC.

Metric Conversion Chart

to convert	to	multiply by
Inches	Centimeters	2.54
Centimeters	Inches	0.4
Feet	Centimeters	30.5
Centimeters	Feet	0.03
Yards	Meters	0.9
Meters	Yards	1.1
Sq. Inches	Sq. Centimeters	6.45
Sq. Centimeters	Sq. Inches	0.16
Sq. Feet	Sq. Meters	0.09
Sq. Meters	Sq. Feet	10.8
Sq. Yards	Sq. Meters	0.8
Sq. Meters	Sq. Yards	1.2
Pounds	Kilograms	0.45
Kilograms	Pounds	2.2
Ounces	Grams	28.4
Grams	Ounces	0.04

About the Author

MaryJo McGraw is a nationally known rubber stamp artist and author whose work has been featured in leading rubber stamp-enthusiast publications. Innovative techniques and creative teaching methods have made her a much sought-after instructor at conventions, retreats, cruises and stores for over fifteen years.

Dedication

To the many paper artists,scrapbookers, rubber stampers and cardmakers I meet around the country at demos, classes and conventions, thank you for your inspiring comments and continuing encouragement.

Acknowledgments

A huge thanks to Krista Hamilton for keeping it all together and in order, Christine Polomsky for the beautiful job she does with laughter and ease, and Tricia Waddell for being so supportive and honest, and for always wanting more!

I would especially like to thank Jenni Bolan of Li'l Davis Designs, Theresa McFadden of FoofaLa and Dave Brethauer of Memory Box for sending me some great products that inspired many card designs. Also, a big thanks to the generous folks at DieCuts with a View.

Thanks to my good friends who always back me up when I feel I am on the verge of bailing out: Shirley Hardee, Elaine Madrid and Debra Valoff. Thanks, ladies.

TABLE OF CONTENTS

RUFF

INTRODUCTION

The explosion of paper products and embellishments in the scrapbook industry is mind-boggling and inspiring.

Walk into any scrapbook store today and you'll find enough cool trinkets, treasures, papers, charms, fibers, ribbons and stickers to decorate so much more than a scrapbook! I focus on greeting cards first and foremost, so these products simply scream quick-and-easy cards to me.

One thing I love about the scrapbook industry is that it offers creative embellishments that are ready to use right out of the package. Adhesives are included or attached, embellishments are available in matching sets, and there are stickers for every occasion you can dream up. Another big plus is that many of the papers are color-coordinated and pre-packaged. Everything is ready to go, which is perfect for cardmaking. Now if they can only make a studio that cleans itself, I'll be set!

With the growing popularity of scrapbooking, stamp stores and other specialty craft retailers are beginning to cross over into the scrapbooking and altered arts categories. Many stores even package their own vintage and retro embellishments that may otherwise be hard to find.

These stores are great places to get information on products and how to use them, meet people who share your interests and find out about the latest techniques and classes.

As always, the bigger craft stores are great sources for general supplies. The kids' crafts section is an excellent place to find inexpensive art supplies when you are just starting out. The Internet is another vast resource for ideas and inspiration. You'll find answers to all your cardmaking questions, information on the latest products, time-saving tips and techniques, craft conventions, online groups and so much more. But perhaps the best resource for inspiration is the world around you. Keep your eyes open for embellishments everywhere, and you will find a world full of fun card ideas waiting around every corner.

In my experience, I have found that there are two types of crafters: one is more literal and follows the materials list and instructions to a tee; the other is more abstract and takes the materials list and instructions as a stepping-off point. In the hopes of appealing to both audiences, I have included specific materials lists and how-to instructions for each project, as well as the patterns I followed to create the cards. Refer to these patterns for the basic layout of the cards, but feel free to incorporate your own favorite papers and embellishments to make them unique.

Getting Started

inspire

Creating handmade cards is easy. With a few basic tools and some fabulous paper, you can create cards that are far better and more personal than anything you could buy ready-made. Starting out on the right foot is very important. More often than not, I find that beginning crafters invest their money in all the wrong places. They buy products they don't know how to use that will sit in the closet until the next yard sale.

This section, which includes a glossary of scrapbooking terms, tools and materials, and some how-to basics, barely scratches the surface. The only real way to learn is to take a few classes, and then practice at home! All the best craft, stamp and scrapbook stores offer excellent classes geared toward every skill level, from basic to advanced. The information you will receive in classes from a good teacher, as well as from the other students, on purchases and organizational ideas alone is invaluable. The money you will save in products you really don't need will more than pay for the classes!

SCRAPPING LINGO

For the best results in scrapbooking and cardmaking, it is important that you understand the lingo. This is so that you will select the right supplies, such as archival quality paper, and correctly follow instructions, such as cropping and embossing. Here are a few terms you should be familiar with before you begin.

Acidic: materials that contain a pH level of less than seven; can fade and damage photos and documents; should not be used on projects intended to last the test of time (more than 50 years)

Acid-free: also called alkaline; materials that contain a pH level of more than seven; safe to use for scrapbook cards and projects

Archival quality: materials that prevent photos and documents from fading and yellowing; the best protection for all projects is to use archival quality products over any other

Collage: any artistic composition made by adhering various materials such as paper, photos and other embellishments together

Cropping: trimming unnecessary images out of a photo

Embossing: applying powder and heat to an area to create a dimensional surface

Gloss: the shiny finish that appears on some paper and photos

Lignin: naturally occurring, acidic substance in wood that breaks down over time; should not be used on scrapbook cards and projects

Lignin-free: materials that contain no lignin; safe for scrapbook cards and projects

Masking: temporarily covering an image to protect it from embellishments such as ink, paint or glue

Matte: the dull finish that appears on some paper and photos

Mounting: adhering a photo or embellishment to another item

pH level: indicates how much acid is in a material; when making scrapbook cards, use products with a pH level of seven or above

Scoring: making a line or depression in paper or cardstock to help it fold (For instructions, see page 14.)

To protect your projects, be sure your cardstock and decorative paper are acid- and lignin-free.

TOOLS & MATERIALS

Here is a list of tools and materials you'll need to create your own greeting cards with scrapbook embellishments. You may already have some of these items around the house. Of course, don't limit yourself to what you see here. Just be sure all the materials you use are acid- and lignin-free. These substances break down the chemicals in photos and papers, causing them to fade, yellow and deteriorate over time. The majority of materials found in scrapbook stores are acid-free, but if you aren't sure just look at the label or ask.

Papers *Paper is an essential ingredient in making scrapbook cards, and the variety of colors, patterns and textures is overwhelming. Coated paper has a smooth texture and does not absorb ink. Uncoated paper has a rough texture and absorbs ink, but is less durable and lower quality.*

Cardstock: This is a general term used for heavier paper, or cover paper. It is available coated or uncoated, in a variety of weights and virtually every color in the rainbow. I always use heavy cardstock (at least 80 lb.), which is sturdier and great for cards. Pre-folded cards are also available, and I have used them for several projects in this book.

Decorative paper: This is available in almost every size, solid color and pattern you can imagine and can be found in any craft store. Messages can be written on it, and it can be cut into shapes, glued to cardstock, decorated or collaged.

Vellum: This light-weight, translucent paper has a matte finish and comes in a variety of colors and designs. It can be placed over paper for a sheer effect, and you can write on it just like regular paper. A glossy material similar to vellum, called acetate, can also be used as a clear or colorful overlay, as in the Belt to Last card on page 122.

Adhesives *A wide variety of adhesives are available for crafting. Here are some of my favorites.*

Dimensional adhesive: This secures items in place and adds dimension at the same time. You can find it in the form of dots (also called pop dots), squares and rolls.

Diamond Glaze: This product, by JudiKins, is my favorite adhesive. A thin layer can be used in place of craft glue to adhere paper to paper, and a thick layer is strong enough to hold most embellishments. Diamond Glaze remains clear when dry, so it can be used over chalk and watercolor paint or under vellum. Unlike other clear-drying adhesives, it can also be mixed with inks, paints and dyes.

Double-sided tape: For good cardmaking, this is a must! I prefer a super-strong paper-lined tape called Mosaic tape. It is great for torn-edge techniques because it tears easily and does not stretch like tape lined with plastic or cellophane. It can even be used with fabric, as you will see in the Bliss card on page 102.

Glue stick: This is great for gluing lightweight objects together.

Photographic masking tape: This is a favorite of mine for use in collage techniques because it gives projects a modern, graphic look. See the Classic Chic card on page 54 for an example.

Repositionable tape: I always keep a roll of this ready for those times when I need an extra hand to hold something in place. It can be lifted and reapplied as desired. Eclipse tape by JudiKins is a wide, repositionable tape I use for masking off specific areas.

Spray adhesive: This sticky spray is helpful for adhering glitter and embellishments, as in Starry Night on page 22. Once it is sprayed, it will remain sticky and must be covered.

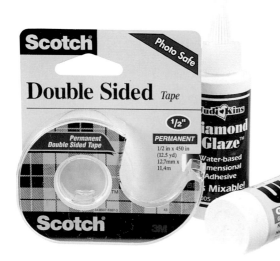

Scotch double-sided tape, JudiKins Diamond Glaze and UHUstic glue sticks can be found in any craft store.

Cutters and Punches
Cutting and punching tools can be used to create backgrounds, borders, mats, shapes and much more.

Clippers: These come in handy for cutting off button shanks, as in the Nostalgia card on page 84.

Craft knife: This sharp blade with a pencil-like handle is used for precise cutting, as well as for scoring a sharp crease. (For instructions, see page 14.) Change the blade often to get the full benefit and safety of the knife. I prefer the X-acto 2000 brand craft knife with a fine point #11 blade, but the smaller, retractable kind are also great because they have thicker blades and seem to last longer.

Corner rounder: This paper punch cuts off sharp corners. I used it to soften the look of the Future card on page 26.

Paper cutters: This is an invaluable tool for cutting large amounts of paper quickly. I have several types at home and use them all, though my favorite is still the old schoolhouse swing-arm cutter.

Paper punches: I often use a simple "anywhere" hole punch that can be positioned anywhere on the paper and then hit with a hammer. Standard hand-held punches also work well and are available in a variety of shapes and sizes. The only problem is that they can go only as far as their arms can reach.

Scissors: These are important tools for cutting paper, ribbon and fabric. Look for a sharp pair of scissors that fit in your hand comfortably. Spring-loaded scissors are available to make cutting easier on your hands, and decorative scissors are also available if you want to add fancy edges to paper and photos.

Self-healing cutting mat: This is a must for serious papercrafters. It will keep your paper from slipping, protect your work surface and save knife blades from constant wear and breakage. An 8½" x 11" (22cm x 28cm) mat is the perfect size for the cards in this book.

Other Tools
These tools, available in any craft store, come in handy when making your own scrapbook cards.

Bone folder: This is a smooth tool shaped like a letter opener and made out of bone (hence the name), wood or resin. Many crafters use it to score a soft crease. (For instructions, see page 14.)

Brushes: I always keep a stiff brush, a soft powder brush and a few paintbrushes on hand for spreading color, removing excess glitter or powder and brushing away metal leaf, as shown in the Heart of Gold card on page 50.

Eyelet setter This tool, which resembles a pen, is used to set tiny embellishments called eyelets. The tapered end is positioned inside the eyelet hole, and the other end is tapped with a small hammer to curl down the sides of the eyelet. (For instructions, see page 15.)

Nail file or sandpaper: This is great for creating texture on decorative paper or cardstock and for filing down elements on embellishments, as shown in the Bamboo Booklace card on page 30.

Pencil and eraser: These are used for marking and erasing measurements and for writing or drawing on your cards.

Ruler: This is a necessity for measuring and cutting. I highly recommend the C-Thru brand clear ruler, which has an embedded metal edge made for craft knife use.

Stylus: Crafters often use this pointed tool for piercing tiny holes and scoring soft creases. (For instructions, see page 14.)

Tweezers: I confess that I used to make fun of folks (sorry) who used tweezers for positioning small items, but I have since had to back off. I can honestly tell you that for positioning stickers and other small items, tweezers work really well.

Xyron machine: This machine, available in craft and scrapbook stores, turns regular paper into stickers. A piece of paper is run through the machine and the adhesive is applied to one side. It can also be used for laminating.

The paper cutter, spring-loaded scissors, craft knife and bone folder shown here are invaluable tools for making scrapbook cards, but they can be used for other crafts as well.

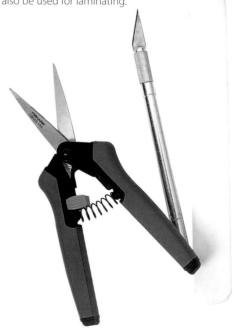

Decorative Embellishments

Use embellishments to add creativity and personal flair to your cards. Below are only a few of the most popular embellishments, but one trip to the scrapbook store and your head will be spinning with all the possibilities! You can also find decorative elements in the least-likely places, like junk drawers, antique shops and flea markets.

Brads and eyelets: These are available in many shapes, sizes and colors. Brads come with bendable prongs that are ready to use, and eyelets must be set with an eyelet setter and small hammer. (For instructions, see page 15.)

Charms, tags, buttons, etc.: These are all supplies that enhance a scrapbook card, including bottle caps, frames, fabric, photos, rhinestones, souvenirs and mementos.

Colored pencils, gel pens, markers and crayons: These are great for writing messages, coloring in images and decorating cards.

Die-cuts: These pre-made paper shapes are available in many shapes, sizes and colors. Die-cutting machines are also available at most scrapbook stores.

Ink: The type of ink you use depends on the look you wish to achieve. Pigment inks are thick, and the colors are vibrant and fade-resistant. They dry slowly and cannot be absorbed into coated paper. Dye inks are thinner, water-based inks that dry quickly and are absorbed into all types of paper. Permanent inks dry by evaporation, not absorption, and are not prone to fading or bleeding.

Stamps: These are always fun embellishments and make cards look great. Buy them at stamp, craft and scrapbook stores, or carve your own out of rubber erasers.

Stickers: The dazzling quantity of stickers is growing every day, and collecting them is no longer just a hobby for kids. They range from simple paper and foil to sewn fabric pieces, plastic pebbles, metal letters and beyond.

Embellish your projects with markers, colored pencils and inks. The more you embellish, the more unique your card will be!

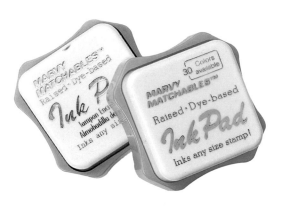

13

BASIC TECHNIQUES

There are a few basic techniques you'll need to know before you begin. These little tricks, which I've picked up over the years, will make every project easier and more enjoyable.

How to Hold Your Tools *Comfort and confidence make all the difference when measuring, cutting and scoring with precision. The photos below demonstrate the correct way to hold your craft knife and ruler.*

Hold Your Craft Knife Like a Pencil

Hold the knife as you would hold a pencil, positioning your fingers as far down the handle as possible. When inserting the blade into the paper, pierce the point of the knife into the surface, then pull the blade down close to the paper.

Keep Your Ruler from Slipping

Place your ring finger and thumb on the outside beveled edges of the ruler, and use your index and middle fingers to hold the ruler in place. This position will keep the ruler from slipping out from under the knife. Sometimes, I also use my pinky finger for balance.

How to Score *Scoring is the process of making a line or depression in paper or cardstock to help it fold. I personally love the sharp crease created by scoring with the back of a craft knife, but some crafters prefer the softer crease made by scoring with a stylus or bone folder. Try them all and see which one you prefer.*

Score a Sharp Crease

To make a sharp crease, place your paper on the cutting mat and align your ruler on the paper along the line where you want your score. Press the back of the craft knife against the edge of the ruler and run along the paper. Fold and crease with your finger.

Score a Soft Crease

To make a softer crease, follow the same process, using a stylus (shown) or bone folder instead of the craft knife.

How to Use & Remove Adhesive Backing
Most of the projects in this book include some kind of adhesive with protective backing, such as double-sided tape or pop dots. Here are a few tricks for removing adhesive backing quickly and easily.

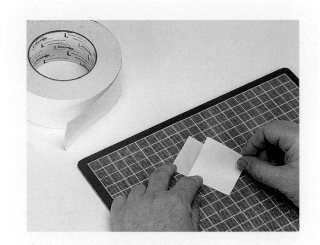

Remove Backing from Double-Sided Tape
Position the tape on the back of the item you wish to adhere, firmly securing it by rubbing it with your fingernail. Gently peel up the corner with your fingernail and pull the backing away from the tape. Never remove the backing before applying the tape to the surface.

Remove Backing from Pop Dots
Sometimes the backing on these dimensional dots is extremely sticky. The best way to remove them is to insert the tip of the knife into the corner of the backing, then pull up with your knife .

How to Set Eyelets
Eyelets are metal or plastic rings that are great for attaching papers and embellishments to your cards. They come in a wide variety of shapes, sizes and materials and must be set in place on a hard surface using an eyelet setter and hammer. In this demonstration, I am setting a round metal eyelet into a small tag, which already has a hole. Use a hole punch the diameter of your eyelet to make a hole if one doesn't already exist.

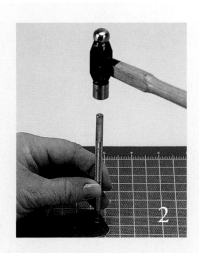

1 **Position Eyelet in Hole** Insert the eyelet through the hole on the front of the paper. Place the paper face down on a hard surface and position the eyelet setter straight up and down with the tip going into the back of the eyelet.

2 **Strike Eyelet with Hammer** Strike the top of the eyelet setter with a hammer, using two or three smooth, even strokes rather than several small taps. The smooth strokes will allow the metal to roll under so that the eyelet sets evenly.

3 **Flatten Against Paper** Remove the eyelet setter and examine the eyelet. The metal should be flat and rolled under evenly. You may need to tap the eyelet itself with the hammer a few times to flatten it.

SIMPLY CHARMING

SO MANY CHARMS, SO LITTLE TIME! Charms are everywhere, and the choices are infinite. New charms are coming out every month! There are so many elements that could be included in this chapter other than traditional metal charms, like bottle caps, metal frames, buttons and clear acrylic shapes. The newer scrapbook charms are excellent because most have their own adhesives attached or included. This is just the beginning of what is available, so think of these projects as a springboard for other ideas.

One consideration in making cards with charms and other three-dimensional embellishments is how difficult they will be to mail. Try to keep items to less than ¼" (0.6cm) thick. Otherwise, you may want to add a few extra stamps and a padded envelope. Better yet, why not deliver them in person!

Bottle Caps

Living in the age of plastic bottles and twist-off caps, bottle caps are so nostalgic. I found these old bottle caps at a thrift store, then added dimensional letter stickers, called sticker pebbles, to update them a bit. If you can't find them in your local thrift store, go to the scrapbook store. Li'l Davis Designs makes adorable bottle caps in pastel, holiday and primary colors, with and without words. They are self-adhesive and sold in packs of six.

Materials

card: 9" × 4" (23cm × 10cm) polka dot cardstock

½" × 4" (1cm × 10cm) orange cardstock

small scrap of decorative paper

sticker pebbles

three bottle caps

pop dots

double-sided tape

craft knife or scissors

ruler

cutting mat

Resources

polka dot cardstock by Memory Box •
orange cardstock by MatchMakers •
sticker pebbles by Sonnets Stamps

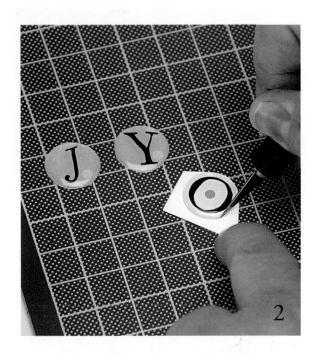

1 **Add Sticker Pebbles** Adhere three sticker pebbles onto a scrap of decorative paper to spell out the word "JOY."

2 **Trim Pebbles** Cut around each sticker pebble with a craft knife to remove excess paper.

3 **Adhere Pebbles to Bottle Caps** Adhere pop dots to the tops of three bottle caps and apply the sticker pebbles over the pop dots.

4 **Score and Fold Card** Place the polka dot cardstock face down in the horizontal position. Measure over 4¼" (11cm) from the right side and score the cardstock vertically. (For instructions, see page 14.) Fold and crease the score.

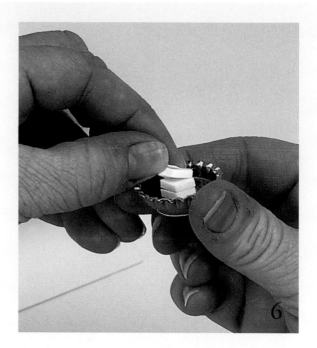

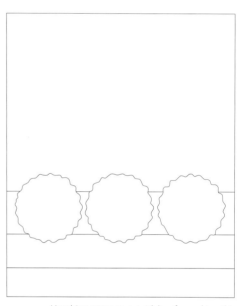

Use this pattern as a guideline for making this card with different papers and embellishments.

5 **Adhere Orange Strip** Use double-sided tape to adhere the orange strip of cardstock across the front of the card, about ¾" (2cm) from the bottom.

6 **Add Pop Dots to Bottle Caps** Stack a few pop dots on top of each other and adhere them to the underside of each bottle cap.

7 **Adhere Bottle Caps to Card** To finish the card, adhere the bottle caps to the orange strip on the front panel of the card.

Admiration

Here is an easy variation using decorative bottle caps with phrases for many occasions. There are stickers available that fit bottle caps perfectly, as well as pre-printed caps like these.

papers	DieCuts with a View Memory Box
bottle caps	Li'l Davis Designs

Do You Love Me?

In this card, I have used some adorable mini bottle caps by my friends at Li'l Davis. By tying on a bit of ribbon, this card makes an excellent gift tag.

papers	DieCuts with a View Memory Box
bottle caps	Li'l Davis Designs

Starry Night

What a wonderful thing spray adhesive is—especially when paired with glitter. Pour the unused glitter right back into the container so you don't waste a sparkle. Spray adhesive is strong enough to hold a wide range of items, including heavy paper, metal charms and small beads. Do remember, though, that wherever it sprays, it stays. In other words, it will remain sticky until it is covered by something.

Materials

card: 10" × 5" (25cm × 13cm) canning jar cardstock folded to 5" × 5" (13cm × 13cm)

3½" × 3½" (9cm × 9cm) dark blue cardstock

4" × 4" (10cm × 10cm) aqua cardstock

metal charm

metal star sprinkles

silver glitter

spray adhesive

double-sided tape

tweezers

Resources

cardstock and metal charm by Memory Box • star sprinkles by Design Ideas

1 **Spray Blue Cardstock** Spray the dark blue cardstock with spray adhesive to cover it.

2 **Adhere Star Sprinkles** Adhere the metal star sprinkles to the sticky cardstock, using tweezers for precise placement and allowing some stars to hang off the edges. Leave space in the center for the metal charm.

3 **Spray Metal Charm** Spray the back of the metal charm with spray adhesive.

4 **Adhere Charm** Adhere the charm to the starry cardstock.

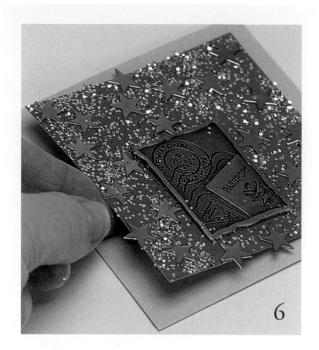

Use this pattern as a guideline for making this card with different papers and embellishments.

5 **Add Glitter** Sprinkle glitter over the cardstock, making sure to cover all the sticky areas that are exposed. Pour the excess glitter back into the container.

6 **Layer Blue and Aqua Cardstock** Apply double-sided tape to one side of the aqua cardstock and adhere the starry cardstock to the center.

7 **Adhere Aqua Cardstock to Card** To finish, apply double-sided tape to the other side of the aqua cardstock and adhere it to the center of the card.

Turning Leaves

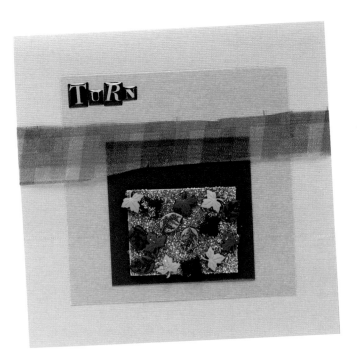

I'm from California, where the weather doesn't change much from season to season. I used little button charms shaped like leaves to re-create the beautiful colors of autumn.

papers	DieCuts with a View
buttons	Jesse James
stickers	Li'l Davis Designs

Better Not Pout

Buttons come in all shapes and sizes, like these snowflake buttons by Jesse James. I stamped the message onto this card, but you can also write with white gel pen or use rub-on letters if you prefer.

papers	Bazzill Basics Paper JudiKins DieCuts with a View
stamp	Making Memories
buttons	Jesse James

you better not pout

Future

Pre-cut window cards make projects like this one quick and easy. The charm I used in this project, a metal frame, fits over the window perfectly. I like using a corner rounder or decorative scissors to soften sharp edges. It transforms a simple straight-edged card into something a little more special. This card would look great with a small school picture or an oversized photo cut down to fit the window. You can also use pre-printed images or clip art if you can't find the right photo.

Materials

card: pre-folded $4\frac{1}{2}" \times 5\frac{1}{2}"$ (11cm × 14cm) kiwi card with $1\frac{1}{4}" \times 1\frac{1}{4}"$ (3cm × 3cm) window

metal sticker

metal frame

$1\frac{1}{2}" \times 1\frac{1}{2}"$ (4cm × 4cm) black and white photo or copy

word sticker

corner rounder or decorative scissors

double-sided tape

craft knife or scissors

tweezers

cutting mat

Resources
*kiwi window card by Memory Box •
metal frame and word sticker by
K&Company • metal sticker by Mrs.
Grossman's*

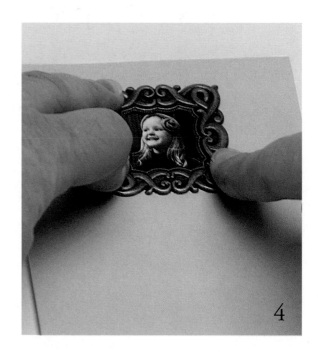

1 **Mark Window Corners** Position the pre-folded card face up on your work surface with the front flap closed. Use the back of your craft knife to mark indentations onto the inside panel at each corner of the window.

2 **Adhere Metal Sticker** Open the card and adhere the metal sticker to the inside panel, using the indentations for placement.

3 **Adhere Photo to Sticker** Apply double-sided tape to the back of the photo and position it in the center of the metal sticker. Press gently to adhere. Close the card.

4 **Adhere Frame to Card** Remove the adhesive backing from the metal frame and position it over the window on the front panel of the card. Press to adhere.

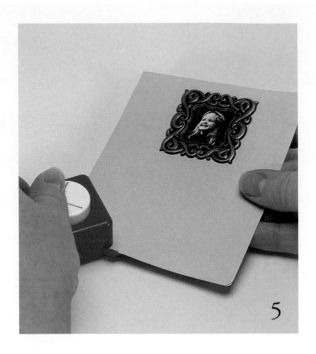

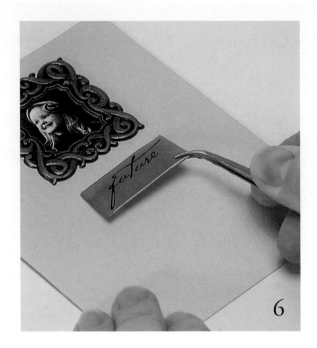

5 **Round Edges** Round the edges of the card with a corner rounder or decorative scissors.

6 **Apply Word Sticker** To finish the card, apply the word sticker below the window.
   Use tweezers for precise placement if desired.

Use this pattern as a guideline for making this card with different papers and embellishments.

Lots of Fun

To make this card a bit more masculine, use strong geometric shapes, a torn edge in the background and plenty of brown! The sticker charm adds a bit of fun, too.

papers	DieCuts with a View
	Hanko Designs
frame	Design Originals
sticker	K&Company

Remembering

Stickers are easy embellishments to add to any card. The metal frame has adhesive on the back, so all you need to do is peel it off, position it over the photo and press!

papers	Making Memories
	Hanko Designs
frame	K&Company
stickers	Pebbles, Inc. (Real Life collection)

Bamboo Booklace

In my little corner of the world, these frames are called booklaces. A strip of paper folded accordion-style makes a tiny book, which is placed inside the frame. When you add a chain or ribbon to the frame, it becomes a fabulous little necklace. Put the two together—book + necklace— and you have a booklace! Add it to the front of a card as a cool gift. The bamboo mat behind it makes a sturdy base.

Materials

card: pre-folded 4½" × 3½" (11cm × 9cm) striped card

6¼" × 1½" (16cm × 4cm) mango paper

¾" × 1⅜" (2cm × 4cm) decorative paper

decorative scrapbook cut-outs

bamboo mat

booklace frame

12" (31cm) piece of yellow seam binding

nail file or sandpaper

double-sided tape

craft knife or scissors

ruler

cutting mat

Resources

striped card by Savvy Stamps • mango paper by Memory Box (Farmer's Market collection) • cut-outs by FoofaLa (Attic Pixies collection) • bamboo mat by Amy's Magic Leaf • booklace frame by ARTchix Studio

1 **Cut Bamboo Mat** Position the bamboo mat on your work surface with the slats running horizontally. Measure approximately 2" (5cm) from the left side of the mat and cut vertically with a craft knife or scissors. Set the smaller piece aside for use in another project.

2 **Sand Sides of Mat** Sand the sides of the remaining piece with a nail file or sandpaper to remove the rough edges.

3 **Score Paper** Position the mango paper vertically, pattern-side up on your work surface and mark it off into 1¼" (3cm) sections. Score and accordion-fold the paper at the marks. (For instructions, see page 14.)

4 **Cut Out Shapes** Position a piece of decorative paper over the cut-outs and cut the shapes out with your craft knife. Cut out a few free-form shapes as well.

5 **Adhere Cutouts** Use small pieces of double-sided tape to adhere the cut-outs to the panels of the accordion paper.

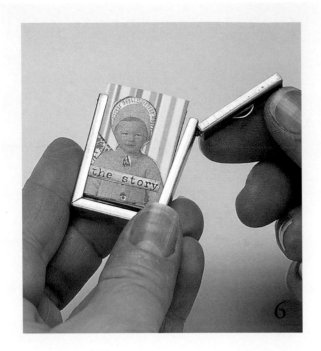

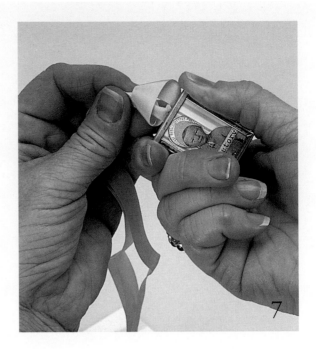

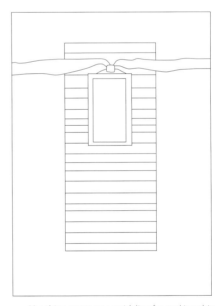

Use this pattern as a guideline for making this card with different papers and embellishments.

6 **Insert Paper Into Frame** Re-fold the accordion paper and insert it into the booklace frame.

7 **Prepare Card and Frame** Apply double-sided tape to the back of the bamboo mat and adhere it to the front of the pre-folded striped card. String both ends of the seam binding through the top of the booklace frame. Feed the ends through the loop in the back and pull taut.

8 **Tie Booklace Around Card** Wrap the ends of the seam binding around the sides of the card and tie them in the back. To finish the card, trim away the excess seam binding, cutting the ends at an angle.

Fun Booklace

Create a quickie little book from a scrap of printed paper and a few mini stickers, slip it inside a booklace frame and this card is complete in no time!

papers	Memory Box
	DieCuts with a View
paper buttons	Memory Makers
bamboo mat	Amy's Magic Leaf
booklace frame	ARTchix Studio
sticker	Pebbles, Inc. (Real Life collection)

Flowers on a Fence

This bamboo mat makes a great lightweight background for many embellishments. Add a few pressed flowers and a vellum envelope, and slip a little necklace charm inside as a gift.

paper	DieCuts with a View
vellum envelope	FoofaLa
bamboo mat	Amy's Magic Leaf
pressed flowers	Pressed Petals

Charming Sophie

This is a sweet photo of my editor Krista's niece, Sophie. Isn't she charming? The first letter in her name is made of a pre-cut acrylic "S." When layered over fancy printed paper and adhered with Diamond Glaze, it creates a cool starting point for the rest of the alphabet stickers. The Diamond Glaze dries clear, so all you will see through the clear letter is the decorative design on the paper. The thinner the layer of Diamond Glaze, the quicker it will dry.

Materials

card: 4¼" × 12 (11cm × 31cm) squash paper folded to 4¼" × 6" (11cm × 5cm)

2" × 2" (5cm × 5cm) brown polka dot cardstock

two 4½" × ½" (11cm × 1cm) strips of brown polka dot cardstock

3¼" × 3¼" (8cm × 8cm) okra paper

1¾" × 1¾" (5cm × 5cm) photo or color copy

acrylic "S"

sticker pebbles

Diamond Glaze

double-sided tape

craft knife or scissors

ruler

cutting mat

Resources

squash and okra paper by Memory Box (Farmer's Market collection) • brown polka dot cardstock by DieCuts with a View • acrylic "S" by Heidi Grace Designs (Glass Effects collection) • sticker pebbles by Sonnets Stamps

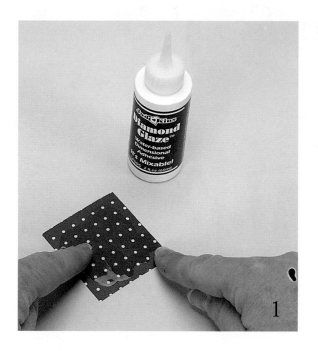

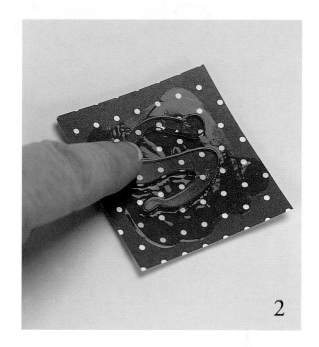

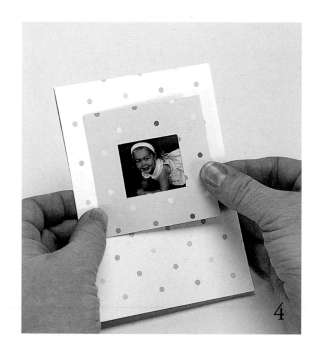

1 **Apply Diamond Glaze** Spread a thin layer of Diamond Glaze over the center of the brown polka dot cardstock square.

2 **Adhere "S" Shape** Apply the "S" over the Diamond Glaze and set it aside to dry for at least five minutes.

3 **Make Frame** Place the okra paper on your work surface and use your craft knife to cut out a 1½" × 1½" (4cm × 4cm) window in the center.

4 **Adhere Photo and Frame** Position the photo so that it is showing through the window and adhere it with double-sided tape. Then, adhere the framed photo to the card.

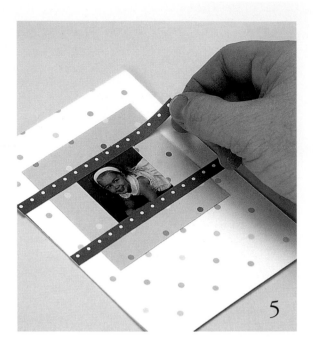

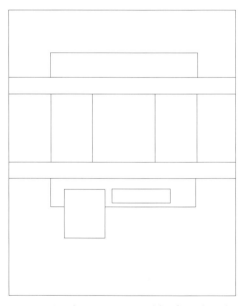

*Use this pattern as a guideline for making this
card with different papers and embellishments.*

5 **Adhere Polka Dot Paper** Use Diamond Glaze to adhere the brown polka dot strips of
cardstock across the front panel of the card, above and below the photo.

6 **Adhere "S"** Retrieve the "S" from step 2 and cut it out with your craft knife. Apply a dab of
Diamond Glaze on the back of the letter and spread it evenly with your finger.

7 **Add Letters** To finish the card, position the "S" on the front panel of the card, near the
bottom. Press firmly to adhere. Trim the sticker pebbles if necessary and adhere them to
the card to spell out the rest of the name. The sticker pebbles are repositionable until firmly
pressed, so don't fret if you drop one in the wrong spot. It will pop right off.

My Little Tori

The metal charm and paper word stickers on this card do a good job of describing my niece Tori, who is full of energy. I wish I could bottle up some of her energy and save it for a rainy day!

paper	DieCuts with a View
stickers	Pebbles, Inc. (Real Life collection) Stampendous!

Chelsea's Smile

This is a great card for using up leftover charms, alphabet stickers and scraps of paper and cardstock.

paper	Memory Box
metal charm	Pioneer
stickers	EK Success

Paperphernalia

PAPER, PAPER, PAPER! I AM HOOKED ON PAPER!
It is a wonderful obsession—an addiction, really. I am unable to stop myself from buying more. Most crafters I meet share my love for all things paper, and yet we all refrain from using it. Why? Because if we use it, we won't have it anymore! So we become paper collectors instead of papercrafters.

This is a tough hurdle to get over, but I will give you a piece of advice that I received from a friend many years ago: There will always be more paper—and stuff in general—for you to buy. And it will be prettier and better than what you have now because your taste will have changed. You will want the newest, freshest things, not the old things you have kept for years.

Keeping this in mind has helped me. I haven't completely stopped collecting paper, but I am finally able to slow down and use what I have and love today, all the while anxiously awaiting what I'll find tomorrow.

Ruff

A pale yellow card can really come to life when you add smaller pieces of striped and polka dot cardstock in bright colors. Top it off with a small square of the same pale yellow cardstock that has been stamped with a cute image like this Scottie dog. Small game tiles also help this card pop. For those of you who don't stamp (yet!), try a graphic element printed on the computer. Or, use clip art or your favorite photo.

Materials

card: 3½" × 10" (9cm × 25cm) pale yellow cardstock folded to 3½" × 5" (8cm × 13cm)

1½" × 1½" (4cm × 4cm) pale yellow cardstock

1¾" × 1¾" (5cm × 5cm) orange polka dot cardstock

3" × 2¼" (8cm × 6cm) green and orange striped cardstock

tile letters

dog stamp

black permanent ink

double-sided tape

tweezers

Resources
cardstock by Memory Box (polka dot and striped cardstock from Farmer's Market collection) • tile letters by West Trim • Scottie dog stamp by Carmen's Veranda • black permanent ink by StazOn

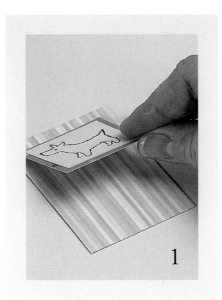

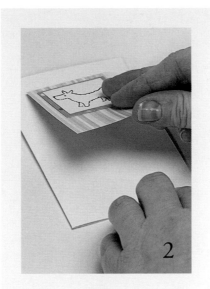

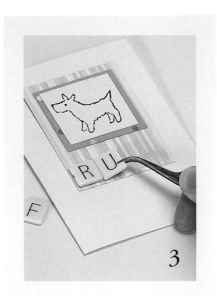

1 **Stamp and Layer Cardstock** Ink the dog stamp with permanent black ink and stamp it onto the square of yellow cardstock, then adhere the stamped cardstock to the center of the orange polka dot cardstock. Use double-sided tape to adhere both pieces to the upper portion of the striped cardstock, as shown.

2 **Adhere Cardstock to Card** Adhere the striped cardstock to the front panel of the card, about ½" (1cm) from the top and centered side to side.

3 **Add Tile Letters** Adhere the tile letters to the lower part of the striped cardstock using small pieces of double-sided tape.

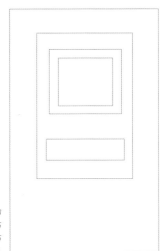

Use this pattern as a guideline for making this card with different papers and embellishments.

Pip the Pup

I have lots of dog stamps, but this one is my favorite because it looks like my Jack Russell terrier, Tapas. Simple stamping in black ink always looks good, especially over layered blocks of paper.

papers	PG
dog stamp	Carmen's Veranda
plaid stamp	Hero Arts
permanent ink	StazOn
stickers	EK Success

Torn Edges

I love the look of torn paper, and this technique gives me a way to use all the bits and pieces of paper I have lying by the paper cutter. Collage is fun, and with coordinating papers it goes so fast. Simply apply double-sided tape to the back of your paper or run it through a Xyron machine to make one side sticky, then begin tearing and layering until you have a nice composition for your card.

Materials

card: $4^{7}/_{8}$" × 7" (12cm × 18cm) charcoal cardstock folded to $4^{7}/_{8}$" × $3^{1}/_{2}$" (12cm × 9cm)

$4^{3}/_{4}$" × $2^{3}/_{4}$" (10cm × 7cm) dark brown cardstock

$^{1}/_{4}$" × $2^{3}/_{4}$" (0.6cm × 7cm) strip of brown paisley cardstock

two pieces of 2" × 6" (5cm × 15cm) cardstock in coordinating colors

$^{1}/_{2}$" × $^{3}/_{4}$" (1cm × 2cm) photo or color copy

$^{1}/_{2}$" × $^{1}/_{2}$" (1cm × 1cm) metal frame

pop dots

double-sided tape

clippers

craft knife or scissors

ruler

Resources

cardstock by Memory Box • metal frame by Card Connection (Charming Thoughts collection)

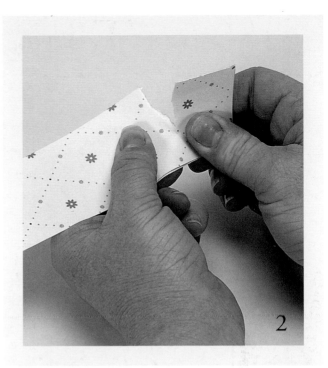

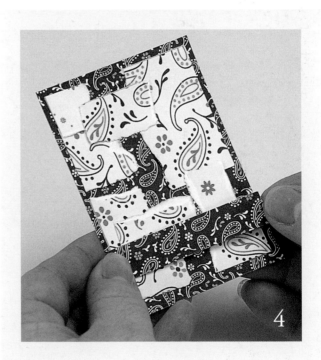

1 **Apply Tape to Cardstock** Apply double-sided tape to one side of both 2" × 6" (5cm × 15cm) pieces of coordinating cardstock.

2 **Tear Cardstock** Tear the taped cardstock into pieces in various shapes and sizes. Remove the backing from the tape.

3 **Adhere Pieces to Brown Cardstock** Adhere some of the torn pieces to the dark brown cardstock, aligning the straight edges of the pieces with the edges of the dark brown cardstock. Overlap as you go, and make sure some of the dark brown cardstock shows through.

4 **Adhere Paisley Cardstock** Adhere the strip of brown paisley cardstock horizontally across the collaged cardstock, about ½" (1cm) from the bottom.

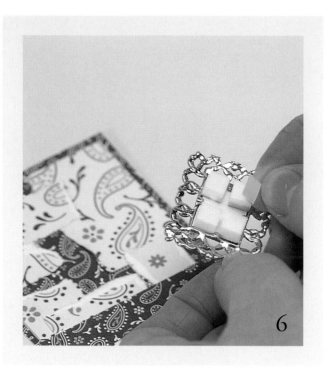

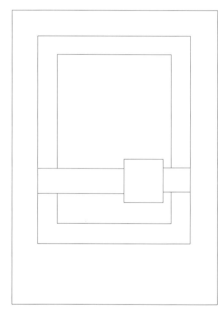

Use this pattern as a guideline for making this card with different papers and embellishments.

5 **Prepare Photo and Frame** Use clippers to cut off the prongs on the metal frame. Trim the photo if necessary and position it inside the frame.

6 **Adhere Frame to Collage** Apply pop dots to the back of the frame on each corner and peel off the backing. Adhere the frame to the collaged cardstock near the bottom right corner, as shown.

7 **Adhere Collage to Card** To finish the card, center the collaged cardstock on the front of the card and adhere with double-sided tape.

Dots and Dashes

Many scrapbook companies have pads of coordinating paper that make this type of card design quick and easy. Pink and brown are such a great color combo.

papers	Making Memories
charm	Coffee Break Design
copper tape	Apropos

Butterfly

I decorated this card with torn pieces of bright butterfly gift wrap. This can be an inexpensive and easy way to add extra elements to a simple collage. The metallic thread adds a lovely elegance.

paper	DieCuts with a View
thread	On the Surface
sticker	EK Success

Spinning Flowers

I found these little metal and paper flowers while I was in Cincinnati shooting the photographs for this book. I thought they were so cute and knew I had to use them. Just a bit of a bend to the petals and poof. They're dimensional! They mix really well with the die-cut paper flowers. I used an eyelet to hold them together, which allows both flowers to spin a bit, as well. Brads work, too, if they are more your style.

Materials

card: 4⅞" × 7" (12cm × 18cm) striped cardstock folded to 4⅞" × 3½" (12cm × 9cm)

2½" × 2½" (6cm × 6cm) pink cardstock

2" × 2" (5cm × 5cm) bird and berry paper

1¼" × 1¼" (4cm × 4cm) bird and berry paper

1½" × 1½" (3cm × 3cm) striped paper

metal and paper flowers

16" (41cm) piece of ½" (1cm) wide decorative ribbon

eyelet

eyelet setter

hole punch

hammer

pop dots

double-sided tape

craft knife or scissors

cutting mat

Resources

striped cardstock and bird and berry paper by Memory Box • pink cardstock by Bazzill Basics Paper • metal flowers by Carolee's (Ting A Ling Accents collection) • paper flowers by Apropos • hole punch by Making Memories

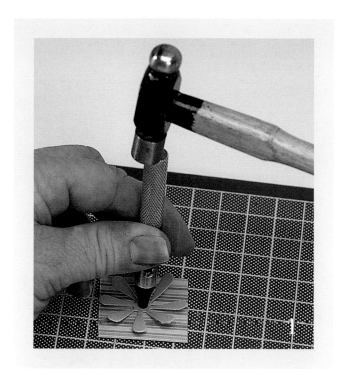

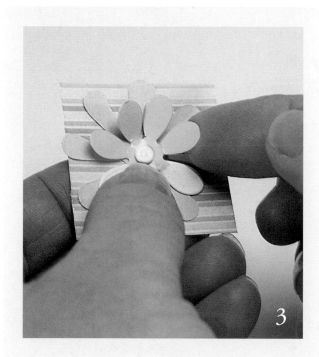

1 **Layer Flowers** Use a hole punch and hammer to make holes in the center of the striped paper and one paper flower. Layer the paper flower over the striped paper, then layer one metal flower over the paper flower, aligning the holes.

2 **Fasten Flowers with Eyelet** Insert an eyelet through the holes, flip the piece over and set the eyelet. (For instructions, see page 15.)

3 **Bend Up Petals** Bend up the petals of the metal flower. Set this piece aside.

4 **Cut Out Leaf** Cut the smaller piece of bird and berry paper into a leaf shape.

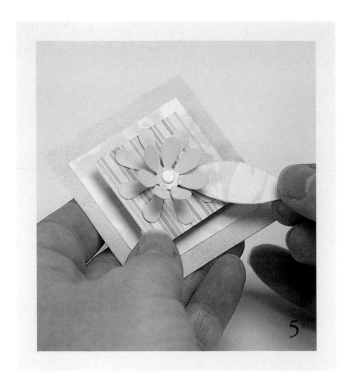

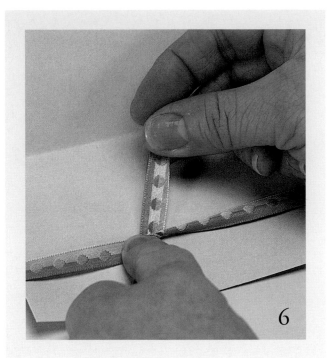

Use the pattern as a guideline for making this card with different papers and embellishments.

5 **Layer Pieces** Layer the larger bird and berry paper over the pink cardstock with double-sided tape. Adhere the layered flower piece from step 3 to the 2" × 2" (5cm × 5cm) piece with four pop dots. Finally, adhere the leaf shape to the small layered flower piece. Set the entire piece aside.

6 **Attach Ribbon** Wrap a piece of ribbon around the front of the card vertically and tie it in a knot on the inside. Trim off any excess.

7 **Add Layered Piece** To finish the card, use double-sided tape to adhere the layered piece from step 5 over the ribbon on the front of the card.

Swinging Heart

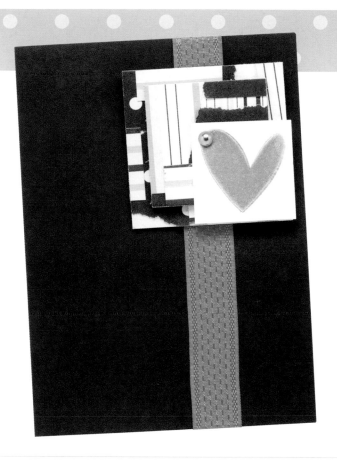

Scraps from previous projects can make up quick squares to layer on this simple little card. You may recognize these scraps from the Dots and Dashes card on page 45.

Papers	Making Memories
seam binding	Thrift store
stamp	JudiKins

Layers of Blooms

Not only did I change the colors on this card to bright green and aqua, but I also positioned the ribbon against the side of the layered squares instead of underneath it. Add a few extra flowers for dimension.

Papers	Memory Box
paper flowers	Apropos
metal flowers	Carolee's (Ting A Ling Accents collection)
eyelet	Coffee Break Design

Heart of Gold

If I ever go off to a desert island, I will take water-soluble crayons with me. I can't live without them. They are super simple to use and very effective for coloring, stamping and so much more. In this project, I used them to add a bit of color to piece of solid cardstock before layering it with metallic leaf. Then I stamped over the design to add even more visual interest.

Materials

card: pre-folded 3½" × 5" (9cm × 13cm) okra card

2" × 3½" (5cm × 9cm) cream cardstock

decorative stamp

wine and terra cotta dye inkpads

metallic leaf

word sticker

water-soluble crayons

paintbrush

stiff powder brush

Diamond Glaze

double-sided tape

craft knife

tweezers

water in small bowl

Resources
okra card by Memory Box • cream cardstock by Bazzill Basics Paper • decorative stamp by JudiKins • inkpads by Marvy • word sticker by K&Company (Life's Journey collection)

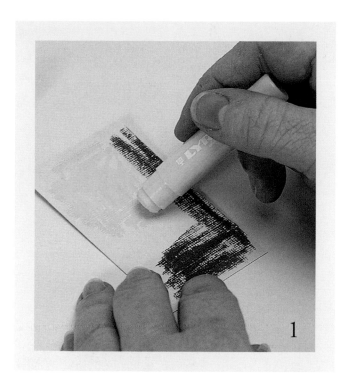

1 **Apply Color to Cardstock** Color the cream cardstock with water-soluble crayons.

2 **Blend Color with Water** Dip a paintbrush in water and blend the crayon over the cardstock. Set it aside to dry for a few minutes.

3 **Apply Diamond Glaze Heart** When the cardstock is dry, apply Diamond Glaze in the shape of a heart. Use the paintbrush to define the shape.

4 **Overlay Metallic Leaf** Gently place a sheet of metallic leaf over the cardstock.

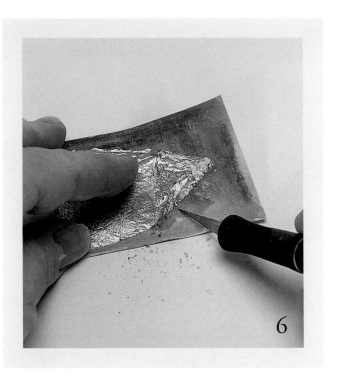

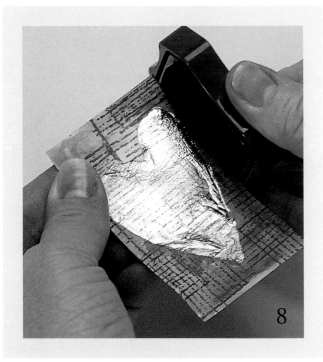

5 Peel Away Excess Leaf Dip the paintbrush in water and brush lightly over the metallic leaf. Peel away the excess and set the cardstock aside to dry overnight. When the cardstock is dry, work away the excess metallic leaf with a stiff brush. (By allowing the foiled piece to dry overnight, you can really rub away the excess foil without the fear of gooey Diamond Glaze ruining the card.)

6 Scrape Away Remaining Leaf Use a craft knife to scrape away any metallic leaf outside the heart.

7 Stamp Image Ink the decorative stamp with terra cotta dye ink and stamp the image onto the cardstock, over the metallic leaf.

8 Edge Cardstock Drag the edges of the cardstock through the wine dye inkpad to color them.

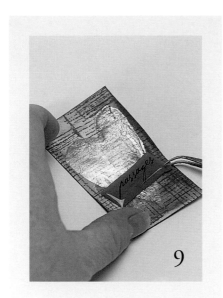

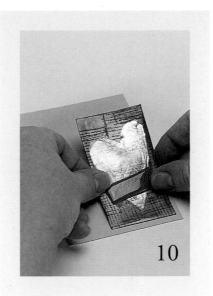

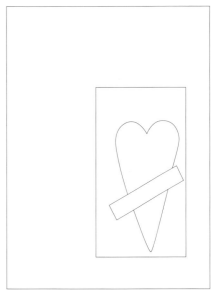

Use this pattern as a guideline for making this card with different papers and embellishments.

9 **Apply Word Sticker** Apply the word sticker to the cardstock over the bottom of the metallic heart, using tweezers for precise placement.

10 **Adhere Cardstock to Card** Using double-sided tape, adhere the cardstock to the bottom right corner of the pre-folded okra card.

Hearts Afire

I used the same water-soluble crayons, foil and stamp for this card, but I changed the paper to make it more contemporary. I also cut out a definition from an old dictionary and used it in place of the sticker.

papers	Savvy Stamps
stamp	JudiKins
inkpads	Marvy

Classic Chic

I love my Xyron machine. It makes papercrafting at home so easy and is worth the investment for paper and vellum lovers. Here is a fun collage project you can try with paper that has been run through a Xyron machine. Machines are available with adhesive, magnetic-back and laminating cartridges and can be found in any craft store. If you don't have a Xyron machine, apply double-sided tape to the back of decorative paper, tear or cut out small pieces and adhere them to the scrap of paper.

Materials

card: 5½" × 8½" (14cm × 22cm) huckleberry cardstock folded to 5½" × 4¼" (14cm × 11cm)

3½" × 5½" (19cm × 14cm) scrap of paper

scraps of decorative paper

metal stickers

paper letters

photo masking tape

Diamond Glaze

double-sided tape

craft knife or scissors

tweezers

Resources

huckleberry cardstock by Memory Box •
metal stickers by Mrs. Grossman's • paper
letters by FoofaLa (Foofabets collection)

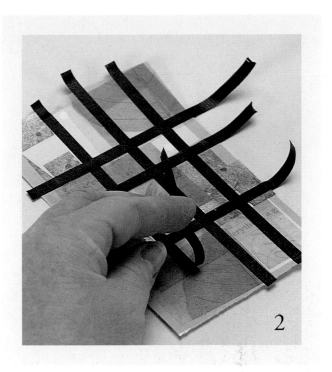

1 **Decorate Scrap Paper** Run scraps of decorative paper through the Xyron machine to make one side sticky, then cut or tear the pieces into free-form shapes. (If you don't have a Xyron machine, use double-sided tape.) Apply paper shapes and metal stickers randomly to a scrap of paper, arranging them in a geometric collage.

2 **Adhere Photo Masking Tape** Adhere strips of photo masking tape over the collage in horizontal and vertical lines. Trim off the excess.

3 **Trim Collage** Use your craft knife to trim the collage to 3½" × 4" (9cm × 10cm).

4 **Adhere Paper Letters** Cut out the paper letters for the word "CHIC" and adhere them to the collage with Diamond Glaze, using tweezers for precise placement.

5 **Adhere Collage** Adhere the collage to the front of the card with double-sided tape.

6 **Make Border** Make a photo masking tape border around the collage piece to frame it. Trim away the excess tape.

Sincerely Yours

Many geometric shapes can be used for taped collages like this one, and a large circle cutter can make the job so much easier! A company called Lion makes the cutter I used for this project. It cuts through cardstock like butter!

Paper	Memory Box
circle cutter	Lion
heart punch	Emaginations
stickers	EK Success

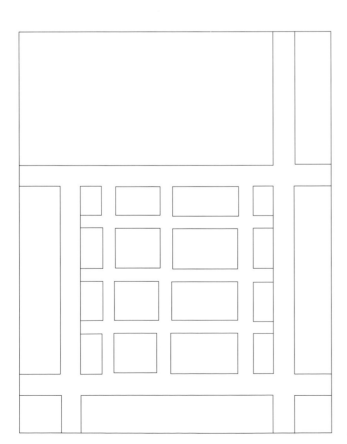

Use this pattern as a guideline for making this card with different papers and embellishments.

Picture This

WE HAVE LOADS OF PHOTOS ALL OVER OUR HOUSE. SOME ARE ON THE COMPUTER, OTHERS ARE IN BOXES, AND THERE ARE STILL A FEW ROLLS OF FILM THAT HAVEN'T BEEN DEVELOPED!

I am always looking for ways to incorporate my photos into cards. As they say, "A picture is worth a thousand words." And with the advantage of being able to see and print out my own photos on the computer, I can size and manipulate them to my heart's content. Digital cameras are becoming more popular, as well, so there's no excuse for a bad picture or missed moment.

Dig out your double prints, or print up a batch of fresh photos, and make something special for your friends and family to enjoy. Combine them with some of the great new paper products and kits available for more personal greetings and mini albums.

Here Kitty Kitty

These little fence cards from Memory Box are so much fun, and they're absolutely perfect for all your leftover double prints. This card features Kiki, the princess of our house. She would never go after as much as a spider, but in this photo she looks pretty fierce. The pressed flowers and green front panel make it look like she is hiding in the grass, ready to pounce on an unsuspecting victim.

Materials

card: pre-folded meadow fence mini card

3¾" × 3½" (10cm × 9cm) black and white photo or copy

pressed flowers

Diamond Glaze

double-sided tape

craft knife or scissors

tweezers

cutting mat

Resources
fence mini card by Memory Box • pressed flowers by Pressed Petals

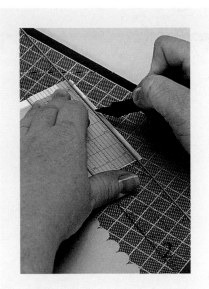

1. **Adhere Photo** Open the fence mini card and adhere the photo to the inside panel with double-sided tape.

2. **Trim Away Excess** Flip the card over and carefully trim away any excess from the photo.

3. **Add Flowers** Close the card and adhere the pressed flowers to the front panel with a tiny bit of Diamond Glaze. Use tweezers for precise placement.

Use this pattern as a guideline for making this card with different papers and embellishments.

Beachcomber

The photo you use can often determine the embellishments, as you see here. For this card, I attached some miniature shells that my daughter and I collected during our trip to the beach. See how easily the front flap transforms into waves?

Fence mini card | Memory Box

Mini Accordion Photo Album

When I saw these pre-packaged, color-coordinated single and double frames, I immediately started thinking of ways to create mini accordion photo albums. The idea came together faster than I expected, and I came up with this fun design. Mix and match a couple of packs in different colors, or cover them with decorative paper for added interest. I have a couple of them sitting on my desk at home.

Materials

card: 3¹⁄₂" × 3¹⁄₂" (9cm × 9cm)
single and double frames

two 3¹⁄₂" × 3¹⁄₂" (9cm × 9cm)
pieces of red cardstock

six 3¹⁄₄" × 3¹⁄₄" (8cm × 8cm)
photos or color copies

embossed metal stickers

sticker pebbles

gold permanent marker

double-sided tape

ribbon or elastic band (optional)

Resources

single and double frames by Design Originals (Mounts and Tags collection) •
red cardstock by DieCuts with a View •
sticker pebbles by Sonnets Stamps •
metal stickers by Stampendous!

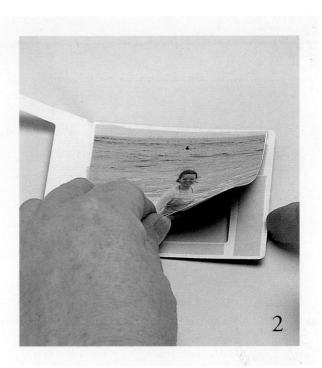

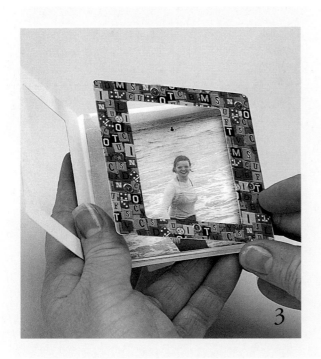

1 **Adhere Photos** Adhere two photos back to back with double-sided tape.

2 **Position Photos in Frame** Apply double-sided tape to the inside right panel of one of the double frames. Center the photos from step 1 inside the frame.

3 **Adhere Frames Together** Apply tape to the inside right panel of the other double frame and adhere it over the photos. You now have a mini accordion photo album.

4 **Add More Photos** Adhere two more photos to the insides of the open frames.

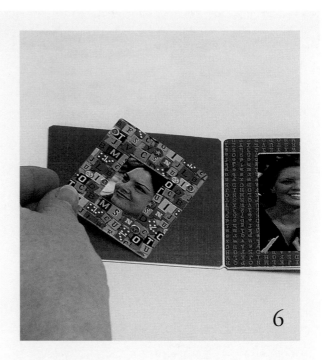

5 **Cover Backs of Open Frames** Adhere the pieces of red cardstock to the backs of the open frames with double-sided tape.

6 **Embellish Frames** Place one of the remaining photos in a single frame and adhere it to the red cardstock with double-sided tape. Repeat with the remaining photo and single frame on the other red cardstock, positioning it diagonally.

7 **Apply Stickers** Apply embossed metal stickers and sticker pebbles to the card as desired.

8 **Finish Card** Edge the sides of the card with a gold permanent marker. To finish the card, accordion-fold it into a booklet and tie with a ribbon or wrap with an elastic band.

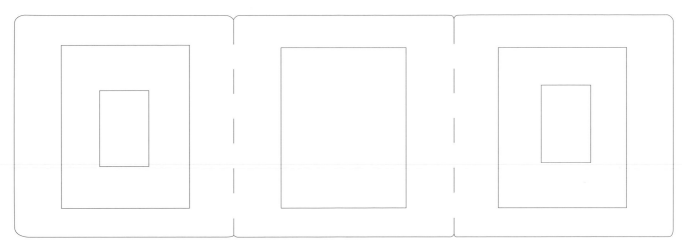

Use this pattern as a guideline for making this card with different papers and embellishments.

Extra! Extra!

I love collecting alphabet stamps and find that these are among the most functional in my collection. To jazz this card up a bit, I stamped letters onto the front with black permanent ink. You can also fold it up and tie it into a nice little package with seam binding, as shown on page 58.

frames	Design Originals (Mounts and Tags collection)
stamps	Postmodern Designs
permanent ink	StazOn

Why So Sad?

I love black and white photos of little kids. This is my niece Tori, whom my daughter photographed at age three in her Grandma's 1940s hat. I love her expression. The photo goes perfectly with the old metal slide frame and a bit of patterned brown acetate. A piece of clear acetate or mica could be substituted if desired.

Materials

card: 4½" × 12" (11cm × 31cm) peach cardstock folded to 4½" × 6" (11cm ×15cm)

acetate

2" × 2" (5cm × 5cm) black and white photo or copy

2" × 2" (5cm × 5cm) metal slide frame

20" (51cm) piece of black and white striped ribbon

rub-on letters

crimping pliers

eyelet setter or tweezers

double-sided tape

craft knife or scissors

ruler

Resources

peach cardstock by Bazzill Basics Paper • acetate by Magic Scraps (Clearly Creative collection) • rub-on letters by Making Memories (Simply Stated collection)

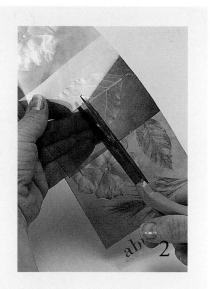

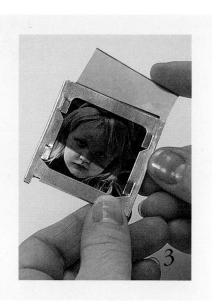

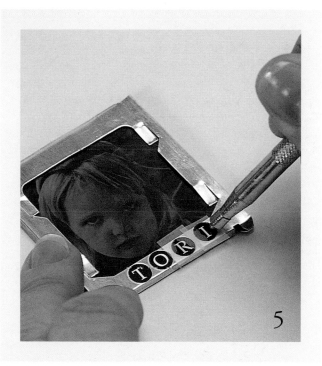

1 **Prepare Photo and Frame** Insert the photo into the slide frame, trimming if necessary.

2 **Cut Out Acetate** Cut out a square of acetate measuring 2" × 2" (5cm × 5cm).

3 **Position Acetate Over Photo** Slide the acetate into the metal slide frame.

4 **Crimp Frame Edges** Use crimping pliers to gently bend in the edges of the metal slide frame to hold the contents in place.

5 **Add Rub-On Letters** Transfer the rub-on letters onto the metal slide frame by rubbing them with the end of an eyelet setter or the blunt end of your tweezers.

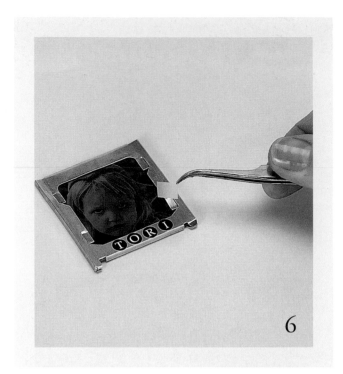

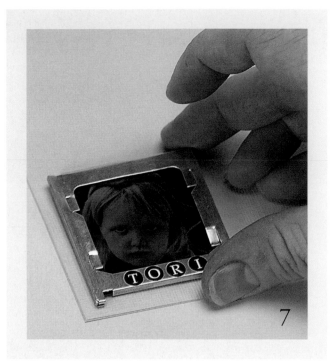

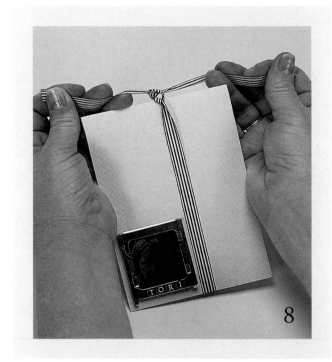

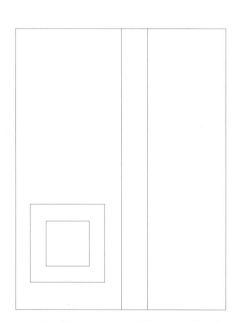

Use this pattern as a guideline for making this card with different papers and embellishments.

6 **Remove Backing** Peel off the backing to reveal the letters.

7 **Adhere Frame to Card** Apply double-sided tape to the back of the metal slide frame and adhere it to the bottom left corner of the card.

8 **Add Ribbon** To finish the card, tie the ribbon around the front of the card and knot it at the top. Cut the ends of the ribbon at an angle.

Tradition

Rub-on letters are available in so many styles and fonts. Fill in areas that didn't transfer with a white gel pen. It is easy to find a style that works for every occasion!

paper	Bazzill Basics Paper
acetate	Magic Scraps
rub-on letters	Making Memories

All Smiles

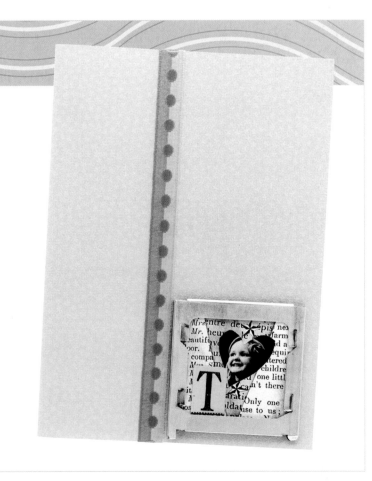

As you can see in this card, the frame can be positioned on either side of the ribbon. It can also be moved to the top of the card if desired. Let your imagination run wild.

paper	Bazzill Basics Paper
paper letter	FoofaLa

Simple Life

People with pets love to get cards with photos of their dogs and cats on them, and it gives everyone else a laugh, too. This card, which doubles as its own envelope, features the infamous Tapas, my Jack Russell terrier. She loves anything shiny, so she usually jumps around whenever we get out the shiny camera. It is hard to get a photo of her standing still, but somehow I managed to capture this cute doggy pose.

1 **Prepare Inside Panel** Open the petal card and adhere the decorative paper square to the inside center with double-sided tape. Layer the photo on top of the decorative paper.

2 **Adhere Tile Letters** Place a ½" × 3¼" (1cm × 8cm) strip of double-sided tape vertically on the left side of the photo and adhere tile letters to spell the word "simple." Close the top flap, side flap, bottom flap and side flap to form a petal shape, as shown on page 70. Press down to secure the photo and letters inside.

3 **Make Paper Band** Wrap the strip of decorative paper around the closed petal card and apply a piece of double-sided tape to fasten it. Do not apply any tape to the card itself so that the paper band can slip on and off easily.

4 **Make Heart Shape** Draw an irregular heart shape on a scrap of red cardstock and cut it out.

5 **Add Rub-On Letters** Transfer the rub-on letters onto the heart by rubbing with your eyelet setter or the blunt end of your tweezers. Peel away the backing and touch up the letters as necessary with a white gel pen.

6 **Adhere Heart to Band** To finish the card, adhere the heart to the front of the band with double-sided tape.

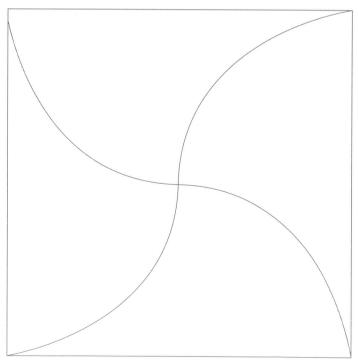

Use this pattern as a guideline for making this card with different papers and embellishments.

For a different look, fold the side petals in first, then the top and bottom petals, as shown here. Wrap the ribbon around the card vertically, attach a few vellum tags and tie into a cute bow. To add a little something extra, decorate the outside of the card with a white gel pen.

petal folder card	Memory Box
paper	Memory Box
vellum tags	Apropos

Vintage photos are my favorites, especially for the holidays. Let the photo shine by simply using a simple printed paper in the background.

Prom Promise

My daughter's prom photos are some of my favorite photos. Here, I have color copied one of the best and created a very girlie card, complete with paper flowers and space inside to include a special message. She will hate it! (Girlie is not her style.) You can add a few pages inside the card to make an album, if desired.

Materials

card: pre-folded 5" × 4¼" (13cm × 11cm) hydrangea window card

10¾" × 5" (27cm × 13cm) blackberry striped cardstock

4" × 4½" (10cm × 11cm) hydrangea cardstock

3½" × 3" (9cm × 8cm) black and white photo or copy

36" (1m) piece of sheer pink ribbon

three vellum heart tags

paper flowers

corner rounder

Diamond Glaze

double-sided tape

craft knife or scissors

scoring tool

ruler

Resources

hydrangea window card, blackberry and hydrangea cardstock by Memory Box • vellum heart tags by Apropos • paper flowers by West Trim

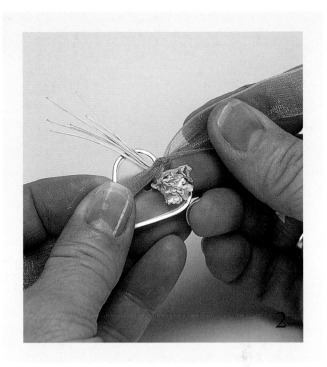

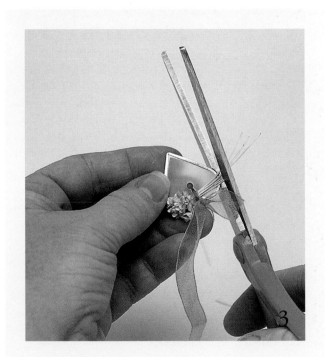

1 **Attach Cardstock to Card** Place the blackberry cardstock decorative-side down on your work surface with the stripes running horizontally. Measure over 5" (13cm) from the left edge, score vertically, fold and crease. (For instructions, see page 14.) Apply strips of double-sided tape to the inside left panel of the window card around the edges of the window. Center the photo in the window. Position the fold of the blackberry cardstock up against the fold of the window card. Close both cards and press to secure.

2 **Attach Flowers and Ribbon to Tag** Trim a piece of ribbon to 12" (31cm) and tie the vellum heart tags to the ends. Tie clusters of paper flowers to the ends of the ribbons. Repeat with one or both of the ends on the remaining 24" (61cm) of ribbon.

3 **Trim Flower Stems** Trim the stems of the paper flowers to about 1" (3cm).

4 **Add Ribbon to Card** Tie the remaining 24" (61cm) of ribbon around the front of the card near the fold, then tie the shorter ribbon from step 2 to the longer ribbon at the top of the card.

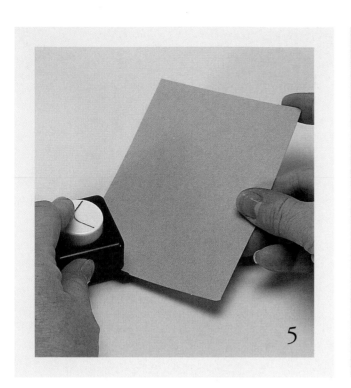

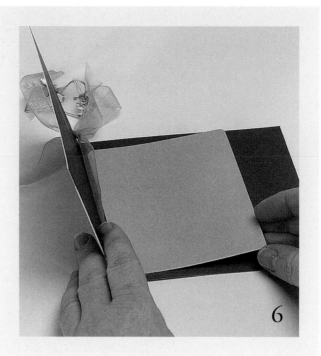

5 **Round Corners of Cardstock** Round the corners of a scrap of hydrangea cardstock with the corner rounder.

6 **Adhere to Inside of Card** Adhere the cardstock to the inside of the card with double-sided tape. This space can be used for writing a personal message.

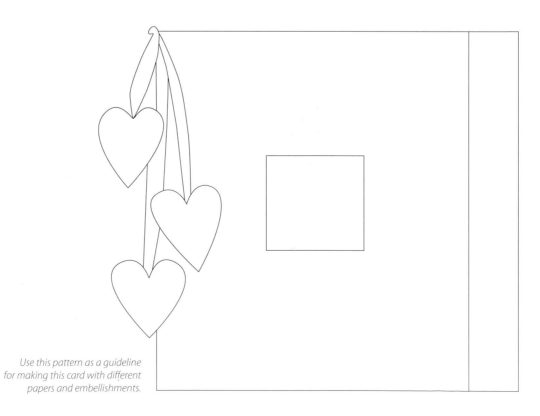

Use this pattern as a guideline for making this card with different papers and embellishments.

Best Friends

Sheer ribbon is always good for feminine cards. Try making a card like this one for a friend's wedding or baby shower. You can cut the window to whatever size you wish.

papers	DieCuts with a View
letter tags	Apropos
stickers	Sonnets Stamps

My Favorite Things

I think my chubby cat, Coco, would appreciate the fact that I cropped her belly out of this picture. Cropping is a great technique for getting rid of unwanted objects in your favorite photos.

papers	Bazzill Basics Paper Memory Box
paper flowers	Apropos
metal flowers	Carolee's (Ting A Ling Accents collection)

Tag, You're It!

NOTHING BURST ONTO THE PAPER ARTS SCENE QUITE LIKE TAGS. They can be subtle or outstanding, playful or purposeful, and they come in a fantastic array of shapes, sizes and colors. Tags are the perfect starting point for handmade cards. They also make interesting trading or business cards and even small books.

You'll find an assortment of tags in scrapbook, craft and office supply stores, from simple manila shipping tags to fancy metal rimmed vellum tags and beyond. Most tags come pre-punched with a standard ⅛" (0.3cm) hole, so eyelets and brads work well. You can also tie them onto cards with ribbon, or use a tag as the card itself. Many stamp stores have die-cutting machines and carry an assortment of tag-shaped templates, which can be cut from any patterned paper or cardstock. They are also available pre-cut and packaged in sets.

Wings and Things

This card pulls double duty as a greeting and a piece of jewelry! Rather than being glued to the card, the acrylic dog tag is attached to the front of the card with an eyelet. After reading the message inside, the lucky recipient can remove the tag from the card, string a chain through the hole and wear it! A metal sticker covers the back to give the piece a finished look.

Materials

card: 5" × 10" (13cm × 26cm) pale yellow cardstock folded to 5" × 5" (13cm × 13cm)

2½" × 5" (6 × 13cm) brown and pink cardstock

die-cut vellum wings in newsprint and white

acrylic dog tag

metal sticker

letter stickers

2" × 1⅛" (5cm × 3cm) photo or copy

eyelet

eyelet setter

hammer

Diamond Glaze

double-sided tape

craft knife or scissors

stylus

tweezers

cutting mat

Resources

pale yellow cardstock by Bazzill Basics Paper • brown and pink cardstock by Making Memories • acrylic dog tag by Coffee Break Design • die-cut wings by FoofaLa • stickers by Mrs. Grossman's

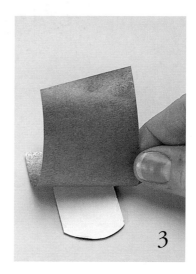

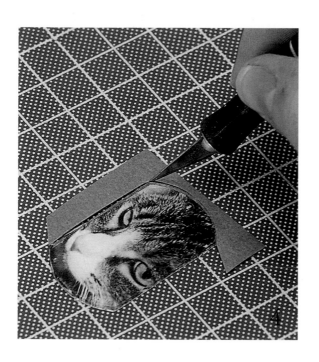

1 **Trim Photo** Use your craft knife or scissors to trim the edges of the photo to match the curves on the top and bottom of the acrylic dog tag. Apply Diamond Glaze to the front of the photo and spread it around with your finger.

2 **Adhere Photo to Tag** Position the dog tag over the photo and press down to adhere.

3 **Apply Metal Sticker** Flip the dog tag over and place a metal sticker on the back of the photo. This will give the tag a more finished look if it is used as a piece of jewelry.

4 **Trim Excess from Photo** Flip the dog tag back over and trim around the sticker with your craft knife or scissors. Use a stylus to pierce a hole through the photo and sticker at the top of the tag.

5 **Adhere Wings** Adhere the newsprint and white vellum wings together with a small dab of Diamond Glaze, off-setting them a little for dimension.

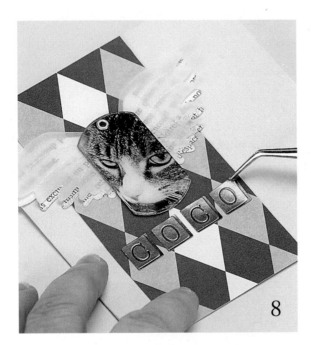

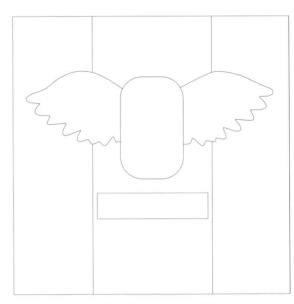

Use this pattern as a guideline for making this card with different papers and embellishments.

6 **Adhere Wings to Tag** Adhere the wings to the back of the dog tag with another dab of Diamond Glaze, making sure not to cover the hole. Set aside to dry for about fifteen minutes.

7 **Pierce Hole and Attach Tag with Eyelet** Use double-sided tape to adhere the brown and pink cardstock to the front of the card, about ½" (1cm) from the fold. Measure down approximately 1" (3cm) from the top center of the card and use a stylus to punch a hole through the cardstock and front panel of the card. Align this hole with the hole on the dog tag, insert an eyelet and set the eyelet. (For instructions, see page 15.) This eyelet will attach the tag to the front of the card.

8 **Add Tag and Letters** To finish the card, add the letter stickers under the dog tag.

Imagine If...

The body of this angel is a square metal edge vellum tag cut on the diagonal. Try extending the use of your embellishments by imagining them in unusual ways. Tags, buttons and stickers can all be used for body bits

papers	Hanko Designs
attic pixies and wings	FoofaLa
vellum tag	Making Memories
sticker	Li'l Davis Designs

Send Me an Angel

FoofaLa offers these ready-made vintage angels, called Attic Babies. Just cut them out and embellish as desired. This card can also be recreated with pictures of your own little attic babies.

papers	Bazzill Basics Paper
attic baby and wings	FoofaLa
stickers	Li'l Davis Designs

Nostalgia

I designed this card to be less frilly and more masculine. The vintage tag sticker really pulls it all together. Add a special recipient's initials to the small tags to personalize the card. Cards like this one are perfect for making ahead of time and storing for upcoming events since they are not created with a specific theme in mind.

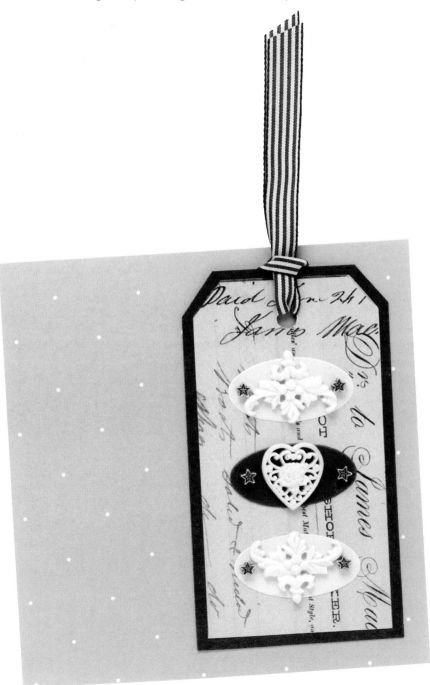

Materials

card: 5" × 10" (13cm × 25cm) blue pin dot cardstock folded to 5" × 5" (13cm × 13cm)

3" × 5" (8cm × 13cm) brown cardstock

vintage tag sticker

three oval paper tags

8" (20cm) piece of black and white striped ribbon

three decorative buttons

tiny star beads

Diamond Glaze

clippers

double-sided tape

craft knife or scissors

ruler

tweezers

cutting mat

Resources

blue pin dot cardstock by Memory Box • brown cardstock by Making Memories • vintage tag sticker by K&Company • oval tags by FoofaLa • ribbon by West Trim

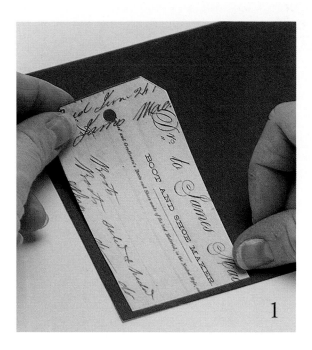

1. **Apply Tag Sticker** Apply the vintage tag sticker to the brown cardstock, ½" (1.3cm) from the left edge and centered top to bottom.

2. **Make Border** Use your craft knife or scissors to trim a ⅛" (0.3cm) border around the sticker.

3. **Add Oval Tags** Glue three tiny oval tags to the front of the tag sticker with a dab of Diamond Glaze. Set aside to dry.

4. **Remove Button Shanks** Use clippers to cut the shanks off three decorative buttons. Or, if desired, leave the button shanks on. Simply punch holes in the paper, insert the shanks into the holes and attach them to the card with glue, wire or fiber.

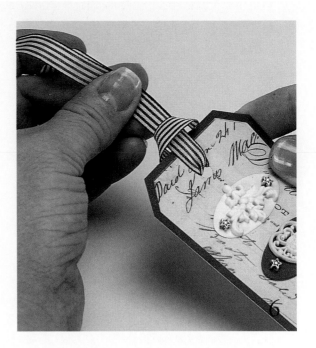

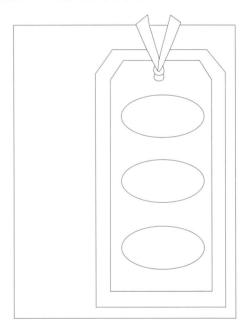

Use this pattern as a guideline for making this card with different papers and embellishments.

5 **Adhere Buttons to Tags** Apply small amounts of Diamond Glaze to the buttons and adhere them to the oval tags. Then, adhere the star beads on both sides of the buttons, using tweezers for precise placement.

6 **Tie Ribbon to Tag** String both ends of the ribbon through the hole in the top of the tag, thread them through the loop and pull the ends to tighten. Trim the ends at an angle.

7 **Adhere Tag to Card** To finish, use double-sided tape to adhere the tag to the front of the card near the right side.

Time Flies

These watch faces may look like stickers, but they are actually real. Li'l Davis Designs sells them pre-packaged with with sticky foam on the back.

cardstock	Memory Box
tag	Apropos
watch faces	Li'l Davis Designs
tag sticker	K&Company

4 You

Stickers create such a professional look, and they make creating cards go so quickly. Use alphabet stickers to personalize any card. I like to mix and match my letters, too.

papers	DieCuts with a View
oval tags	FoofaLa
stickers	Li'l Davis Designs

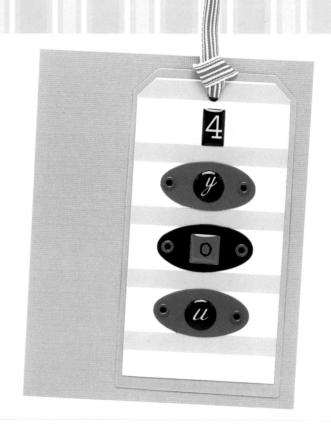

Pocket Tag

Large tags are exceptional for creating mini pockets that hold secret messages. By simply folding up the bottom section of a large tag, a pocket can be formed. In this project, I have inserted a metal-rimmed vellum tag and a couple of small paper scraps from another project into the pocket. The pocket is also great for holding money and gift certificates for lucky recipients.

Materials

card: pre-folded 3½" × 7" (9cm × 18cm) green tag card

5" × 2½" (13cm × 6cm) black tag

5" × 2½" (13cm × 6cm) brown tag

5" × 2½" (13cm × 6cm) beige tag

decorative vellum

round vellum tag with metal frame

scraps of decorative cardstock

heart paper punch

24" (61cm) piece of white string

Diamond Glaze

double-sided tape

craft knife or scissors

ruler

cutting mat

Resources

green tag card by Memory Box • black, brown and beige tags by FoofaLa (Tags to Go collection) • decorative vellum and cardstock by K&Company (Stamp Collage collection) • heart paper punch by Emaginations

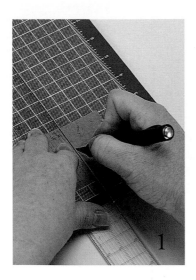

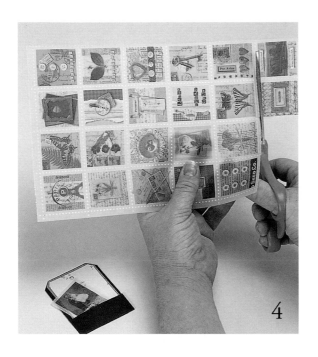

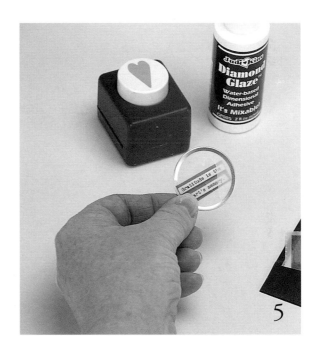

1 **Cut Tags** Use a craft knife or scissors to cut the beige tag to 3" x 2¼" (8cm x 6cm) and the brown tag to ¼" (0.6cm) larger on all sides. Angle the top edges as shown on page 88.

2 **Layer Tags** Use double-sided tape to adhere the beige tag to the brown tag and the brown tag to the black tag, aligning the holes on each tag.

3 **Make Pocket Tag** Score the black tag horizontally 3¼" (8cm) from the bottom. (For instructions, see page 14.) Cut off ½" (1cm) from the bottom, add thin strips of double-sided tape to each side, fold and crease the score to make a pocket.

4 **Fill Pocket** Use a craft knife or scissors to cut two shapes out of the decorative vellum. Tuck them into the pocket and add a tiny dab of Diamond Glaze to secure.

5 **Decorate Vellum Tag** Use the heart paper punch to punch out the center of the round vellum tag. Cut out a small scrap of decorative vellum and adhere it to the center of the tag with a dab of Diamond Glaze. Insert the tag into the pocket.

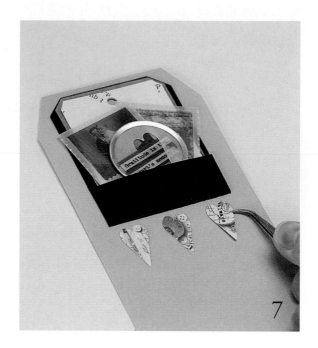

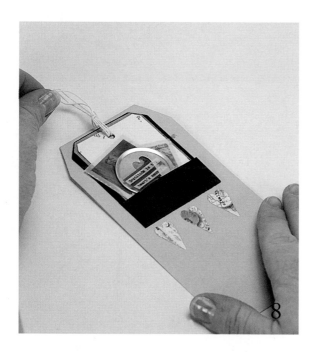

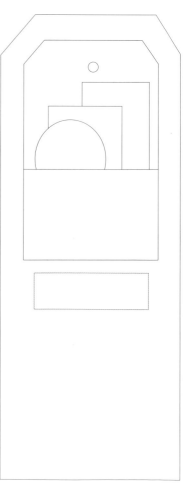

6 **Adhere Pocket Tag to Card** Use double-sided tape to adhere the black pocket tag to the front of the green tag card, aligning the holes at the top.

7 **Add Hearts to Card** Punch three hearts out of scraps of decorative cardstock. Apply a small amount of Diamond Glaze to the backs of the hearts and adhere them to the card below the layered pocket tag.

8 **Finish with String** To finish the card, tie a piece of string to the top of the tag through the holes.

Use this pattern as a guideline for making this card with different papers and embellishments.

Sentiments

I transferred rub-on letters onto a vellum tag for this simple and sweet card. Instead of ribbon, thread a tiny strip of paper through the holes at the top.

papers	Memory Box
vellum tag	Making Memories
rub-on letters	Simply Stated

Be Mine

Tiny strips of torn fabric make great embellishments for graphic cards like this one. The rough edges of the fabric are a nice contrast to the bold colors and simple shapes on the card. Tuck a little note inside the pocket for someone special!

tag card	Memory Box
papers	Bazzill Basics Paper
	FoofaLa

Ooh La La

This is my favorite card in the book! The flowers are so fresh, and the copper tags and rhinestones are the perfect mix of retro and glam. I also used glitter glue, the multi-tasker of all craft supplies, to adhere the rhinestones and add a little sparkle to the card. The glue dries clear and all you're left with is the shine!

Materials

card: $4^{1}/_{4}" \times 5^{1}/_{2}"$ (11cm × 14cm) pink tag card

$4" \times 4^{1}/_{2}"$ (10cm × 11cm) flower paper

three metal tags

paper flowers

letter decals

rhinestone crystals

glitter glue

Diamond Glaze

double-sided tape

eyelet setter or tweezers

ruler

Resources

pink tag card by Memory Box • flower paper by Francis Meyer • metal tags by FoofaLa • paper flowers by Apropos • letter decals by Creative Imaginations

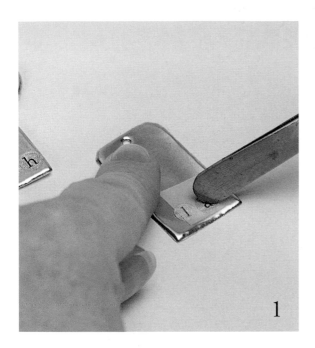

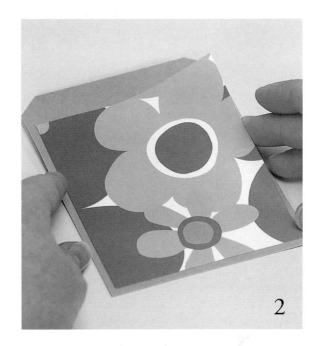

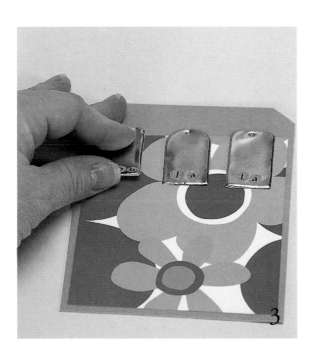

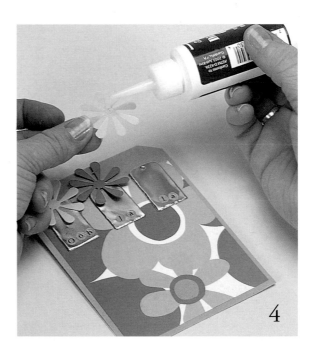

1. **Adhere Rub-On Letters** Place letter decals spelling the words "Ooh la la" on the bottoms of three metal tags. Rub the letters with the end of your eyelet setter or tweezers to transfer them onto the tags. Be careful when transferring the letters, as they are very sticky.

2. **Attach Decorative Paper** Using double-sided tape, attach the flower paper to the front of the pink tag card, about ⅛" (.03cm) from the bottom and centered side-to-side.

3. **Apply Metal Tags** Peel the protective strips from the backs of the metal tags and adhere the tags to the flower paper, about ¾" (2cm) from the top of the card. The edges of the metal tags can be very sharp, so be careful.

4. **Add Paper Flowers** Place a tiny drop of Diamond Glaze on the back center of three paper flowers. Position the flower centers over the holes on the metal tags and press them down to adhere.

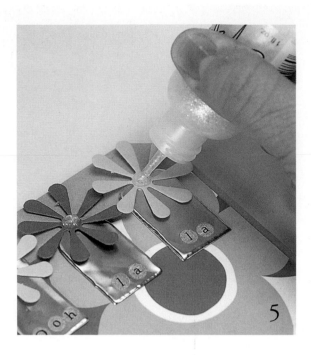

5 **Apply Glitter Glue** Add a small drop of glitter glue to the center of each flower.

6 **Adhere Rhinestones** To finish the card, adhere a few tiny rhinestone crystals on each dot of glitter glue, using tweezers for precise placement.

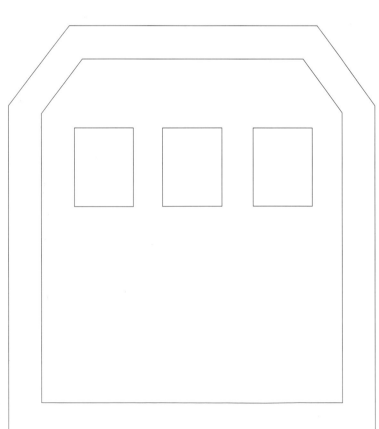

Use this pattern as a guideline for making this card with different papers and embellishments.

Bon Voyage

I have always loved these swirly paper clips, and now Clipiola makes them in a bunch of fun colors. Add them to a pre-folded tag card like this one by DieCuts with a View.

tag card	DieCuts with a View
clips	Clipiola
tags	Design Originals
stickers	Li'l Davis Designs K&Company

A Wink & a Smile

I glued antique poker chips to the top of this tag card, then embellished them with letter stickers by Li'l Davis. I got the quote from a product called quote stacks, which are quotes that have been pre-printed on vellum, made by DieCuts with a View. I love layering them over decorative paper.

tag card and quote stack	DieCuts with a View
stickers	Li'l Davis Designs

Easy as 1-2-3

The bottle caps and old newsprint letters on this card add a vintage feel. I really like how it turned out set against the black and white striped background. And the vellum tags give it just the right amount of flair. Wouldn't it be a great tag to put on a gift for an artsy friend or teenager?

Materials

card: pre-folded 3½" × 5" (9cm × 13cm) black and white striped card

two vellum tag stickers

paper letters

three small bottle caps

24" (61cm) piece of beige string

pop dots

double-sided tape

craft knife or scissors

ruler

cutting mat

Resources

striped card by Savvy Stamps ● vellum tag stickers by Stickopatomus ● paper letters by FoofaLa ● bottle caps by Li'l Davis Designs

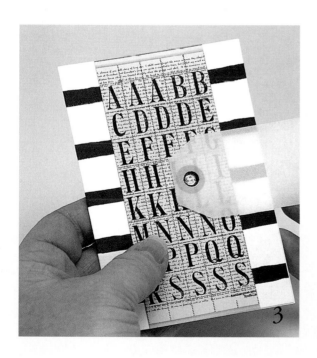

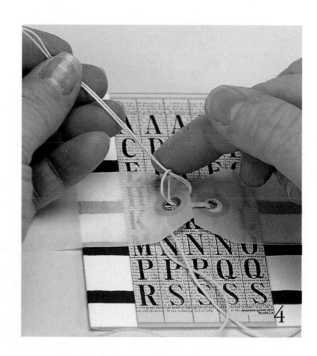

1 **Trim Paper Letters** Use a craft knife or scissors to trim a block of paper letters to measure 2⅛" × 5" (5cm × 13cm).

2 **Apply Letters** Apply a strip of double-sided tape to the back of the letters and center them on the front of the card.

3 **Adhere Vellum Tags** Remove the backings from the vellum tag stickers and position the tags across the front of the card with the tops pointing inward and touching in the center.

4 **Add Ribbon to Tags** Before pressing down to adhere the tags, cut the string in half and thread both pieces through the holes in the tags. Press the tags down firmly and tie the strings in a knot on the front of the card.

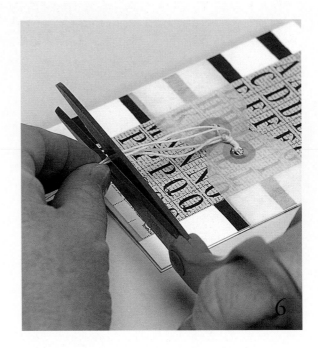

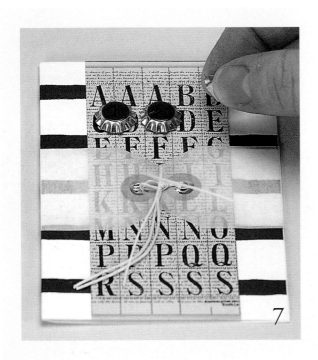

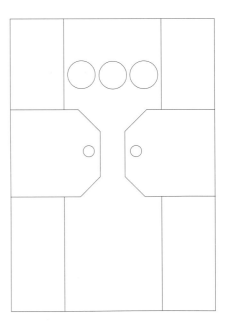

Use this pattern as a guideline for making this card with different papers and embellishments.

5 **Trim Excess from Tags** Flip the card over and trim off the excess from the vellum tag stickers.

6 **Trim Strings** Trim the strings to the length of the card.

7 **Adhere Bottle Caps** To finish the card, apply pop dots to the backs of three tiny bottle caps. Align the caps under the first row of letters, just above the vellum tag stickers.

Fashionista

Adding fancy embellishments like these antique silver shoe charms really makes a basic design pop! I tied them onto the card with a piece of black stretchy cord.

tag stickers	K&Company
papers	K& Company
	Bazzill Basics Paper

How Cute

Two tags can create a cute trim for the front of a card by simply positioning the holes on the tops of the tags pointing toward each other. Trim the excess from the edges of the card with a craft knife.

papers	Bazzill Basics Paper
	DieCuts with a View
button tags	EK Success
wooden letters	Li'l Davis Designs

Buttons And Bows

BUTTONS, RIBBONS, FABRIC AND OTHER SEWING EMBELLISHMENTS, CALLED "NOTIONS" WAY BACK WHEN, used to be readily available in the notions section of every department store in town. Of course, those were the days when everyone still sewed and mended. These days, notions are found in scrapbook, stamp and craft stores, and no sewing is required. Many notions come with adhesives already on the back. Likewise, buttons can be adhered to paper with a thin layer of Diamond Glaze, and ribbon can be tied to a card with a knot or bow. I especially like seam binding, which is often used in sewing as trim, because it is cheaper and sturdier than ribbon. It comes in every color imaginable.

Don't let the title of this chapter fool you. There are so many notions available besides buttons and bows, including snaps, eyelets and zippers. Look through thrift store clothing for unique buttons, old scarves and antique ribbons. You have millions of items to choose from, and I recommend buying the best you can afford. They go on sale at craft stores often, so stock up when you can!

Bliss

When I discovered how well Mosaic tape works with fabric, I started incorporating it into lots of cards. This paper-lined tape tears easily and does not stretch like tape lined with plastic or cellophane. I love the look of fabric with frayed edges, so I purposefully tear the ends, then pull out even more threads from the sides. If you prefer cleaner edges, simply fold them under and iron them down to make a stiff crease.

Materials

card: 6½" × 8" (17cm × 20cm)
aqua cardstock folded to
3¼" × 8" (8cm × 20cm)

vellum heart tag

dimensional letter stickers

assorted buttons

assorted plaid fabrics

Diamond Glaze

double-sided tape

craft knife or scissors

clippers

ruler

tweezers

Resources

aqua cardstock by Memory Box • vellum heart tag by Apropos • stickers by Making Memories (Page Pebbles collection)

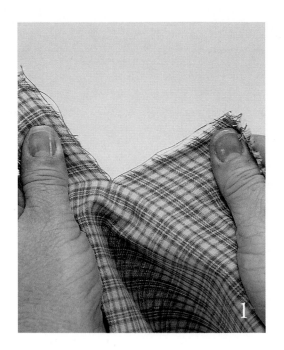

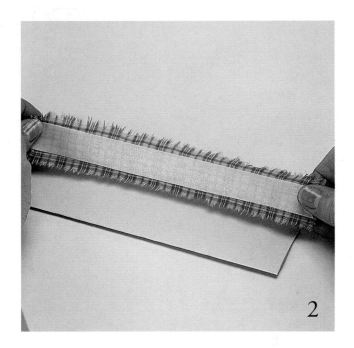

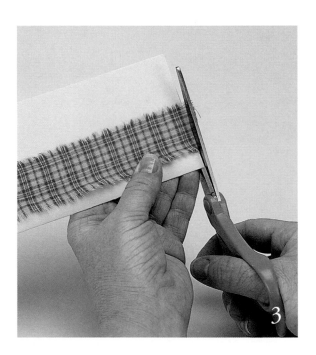

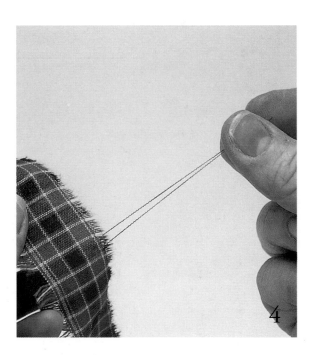

1   **Fray Fabric Edges** Tear a strip of fabric to approximately 1" × 8½" (3cm × 22cm). Pull out a few additional fibers for a frayed look.

2   **Adhere Fabric to Card** Position the card with the front flap closed and the fold pointing to the left. Apply double-sided tape to the back of the fabric strip and adhere it vertically to the front of the card, about ½" (1cm) from the fold.

3   **Trim Excess Fabric** Use scissors to trim the excess fabric from the top and bottom of the card.

4   **Add More Fabric** Tear a second strip of fabric to ½" × 8½" (1cm × 22cm) and a third strip to 1" × 3¼" (3cm × 8cm). Pull out more fibers on the sides, as shown. Adhere the second strip on top of the first strip, then adhere the third strip across the card horizontally, about 1¼" (3cm) from the top. Trim the excess.

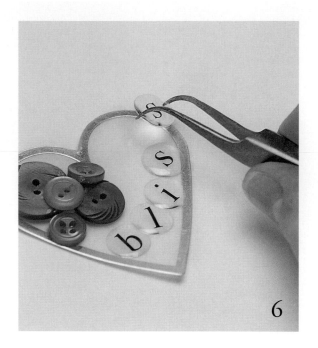

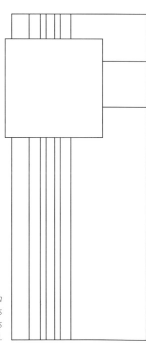

Use this pattern as a guideline for making this card with different papers and embellishments.

5 **Adhere Buttons** Adhere several buttons to the vellum heart tag with Diamond Glaze. Diamond Glaze works great with vellum because it dries clear.

6 **Apply Letter Stickers** Apply dimensional letter stickers to the tag, spelling the word "bliss" and using tweezers for precise placement.

7 **Adhere Tag** To finish the card, cut a tiny scrap of fabric no larger than ½" (1cm) wide and tie it through the hole in the top of the vellum heart tag. Apply Diamond Glaze to the fabric on the card and adhere the tag.

True Love

Here is an example of how several very different fabrics can complement each other so well. I layered a piece of fabric with frayed edges over a piece with straight edges to add more interest.

paper	DieCuts with a View
vellum tag	Making Memories
tag sticker	Pebbles, Inc. (Real Life collection)
love sticker	K&Company

Counting on You

You can find crazy fabrics just about anywhere. Go through the old rag bag and you'll be amazed at what you might find. Here, I used up leftover number stickers to decorate a long, thin vellum tag. This card is perfect for a birthday or anniversary.

paper	DieCuts with a View
buckle and vellum tag	Making Memories
stickers	Pioneer

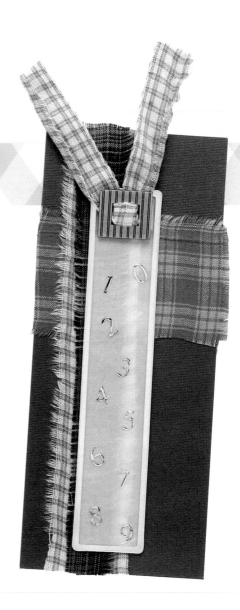

Velvet Blooms

This card turns two separate window cards into one tri-fold card, and the front and middle flaps both have windows. The beautiful velvet blossoms make a bright and bold statement. You can substitute them for other fabric flowers or use silk, paper or real pressed flowers for a different look.

Materials

card: pre-folded 4¾" × 4¾" (12cm × 12cm) pale green card with pre-cut 1½" × 1½" (4cm × 4cm) window

card: pre-folded 4¾" × 4¾" (12cm × 12cm) dark green card with pre-cut 1½" × 1½" (4cm × 4cm) window

½" × ½" (1cm × 1cm) plaid fabric

12" (30cm) piece of ½" (1cm) wide decorative ribbon

velvet flowers

photo or color copy (optional)

Diamond Glaze

double-sided tape

craft knife or scissors

ruler

cutting mat

Resources
pale green and dark green window cards by Memory Box • velvet flowers by Apropos

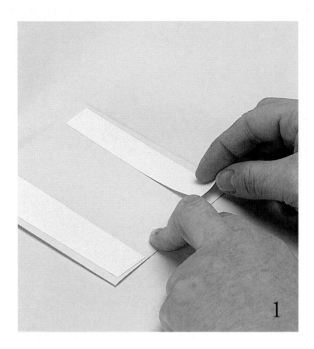

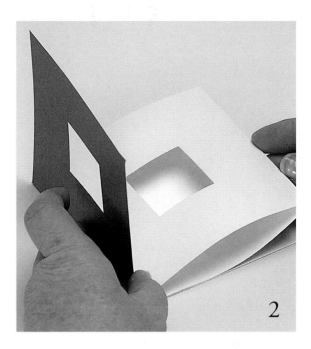

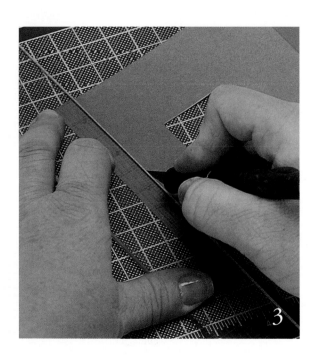

1   **Apply Tape to Card** Apply double-sided tape to the back of the pale green card.

2   **Join Cards to Form Tri-Fold Card** Position the opening of the pale green card into the fold of the dark green card. Close the dark green card to adhere. You now have a tri-fold card with the dark green window flap overlapping the pale green window flap.

3   **Trim Front Flap** Use a craft knife or scissors to trim ½" (1cm) from the right edge of the dark green front flap.

4   **Make Window Marks and Apply Fabric** Close the pale green flap, then the dark green flap. Use the back of your craft knife to make light indentations on the inside panel at the inside edges of the window. Open both flaps and adhere a square of fabric to the inside panel, using the indentations for placement.

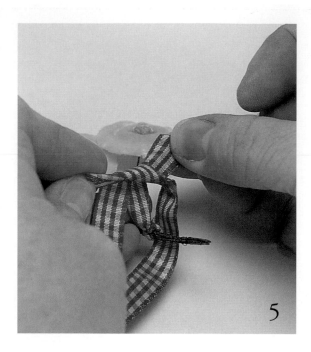

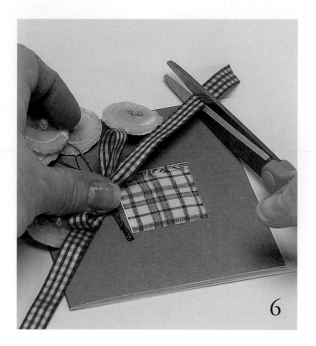

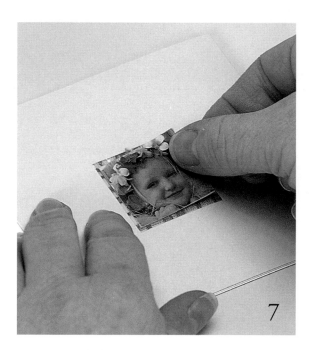

5 **Tie Bow Around Stems** Wrap a piece of ribbon around a bundle of velvet flowers and tie it in a bow.

6 **Adhere Flower Bundle to Card** Close the card and adhere the flower bundle to the left of the window with Diamond Glaze. Trim the ribbon ends so they are even with the sides. Send the card as is, or continue with the next step if desired.

7 **Adhere Photo** Trim a photo or color copy to slightly smaller than the fabric square and adhere it over the fabric with double-sided tape.

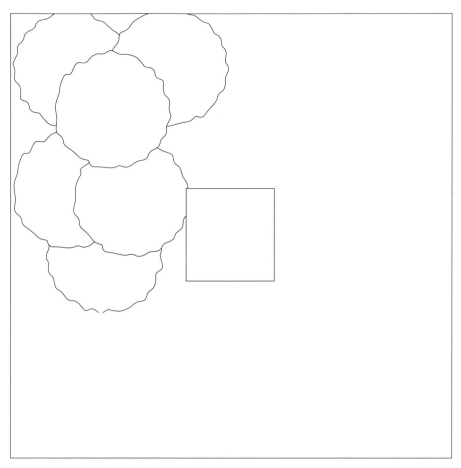

Use this pattern as a guideline for making this card with different papers and embellishments.

Freckles

What a face! Add a few fancy fabric flowers, sticker letters and you're done! This card would also look great in black and white with a few small silk daisies.

papers	Bazzill Basics Paper DieCuts with a View
flowers	The Card Connection
stickers	K&Company

Hugs and Kisses

Remember these little paper flowers? I used them a lot as a kid on many projects, and I still enjoy working with them as an adult. Keeping things simple, these pre-cut window cards make any project a speedy one. The organdy bag adds a frilly touch, and the buttons already have adhesives on the backs, so they are ready to be positioned on the card.

Materials

card: 5" × 10" (13cm × 25cm) pale pink cardstock folded to 5" × 5" (13cm × 13cm)

pre-folded 4³/₄" × 4³/₄" (12cm × 2cm) plum card with pre-cut 1¹/₂" × 1¹/₂" (4cm × 4cm) window

small organdy bag

paper flowers

adhesive buttons

metal stickers

Diamond Glaze

double-sided tape

craft knife or scissors

ruler

Resources

pale pink cardstock by Bazzill Basics Paper • plum window card by Memory Box • paper flowers by Apropos • adhesive buttons by EK Success (Laura Ashley collection) • metal stickers by EK Success (Inspirations collection)

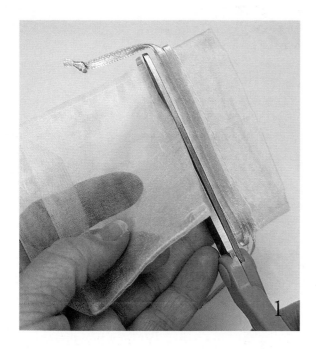

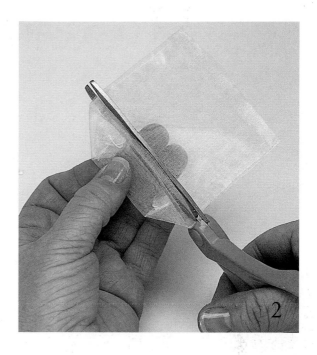

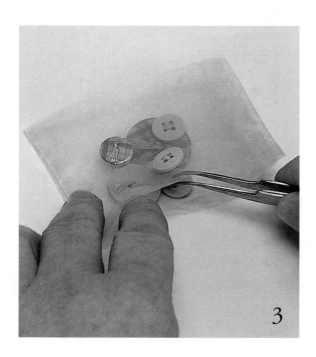

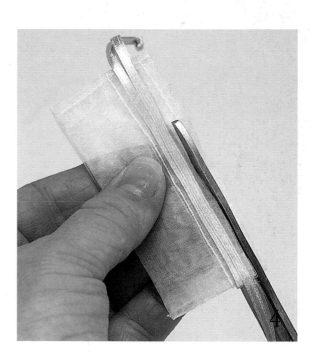

1 **Cut Top Off Bag** Use scissors to cut the top off the organdy bag, just under the stitching.

2 **Cut Bottom Off Bag** Cut off the bottom of the bag, just above the folds, to create a 2½" (6cm) wide organdy tube.

3 **Add Buttons to Bag** Adhere several buttons inside and on top of the organdy tube.

4 **Remove Ribbon** Retrieve the top piece of the bag from step 1 and cut above the seam to remove the ribbon. Be careful not to cut the ribbon, as you will use it in step 6.

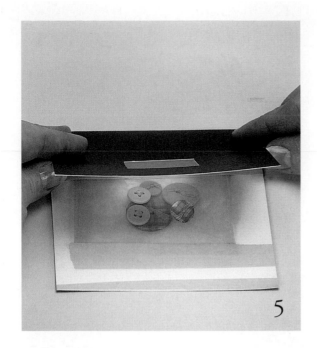

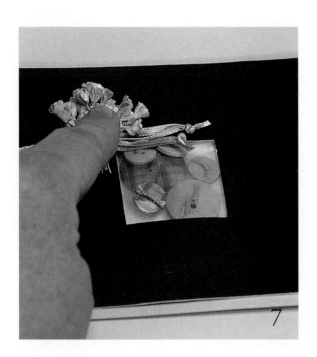

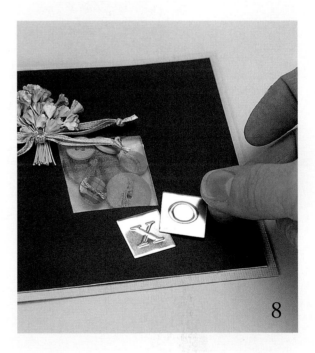

5 **Adhere Bag and Close Card** Open the plum card flap to the top. Apply a small piece of double-sided tape to the back of the organdy tube and center it on the inside back panel of the card. Use thin strips of double-sided tape to close the ends of the bag. Then, apply several thin strips of tape to the inside bottom edge of the card. Remove the backing, close the card and press down to secure.

6 **Tie Ribbon to Flowers** Tie knots at the ends of the ribbon, then tie it around a bundle of paper flowers. Trim the stems to 1" (3cm).

7 **Adhere to Card and Add Flowers** Adhere the plum card to the center of the light pink card with double-sided tape, then adhere the flower bundle to the plum card at the top left corner of the window with Diamond Glaze.

8 **Add Stickers** Add "X" and "O" stickers to the plum card at the bottom right corner of the window.

Fleur

I used wooden flowers instead of buttons in this card, and a sheer fabric to encase them. Remember, when you add more than ¼" (0.6cm) thickness to any card, it will need extra postage.

papers	Bazzill Basics Paper DieCuts with a View
flowers and letters	Li'l Davis Designs

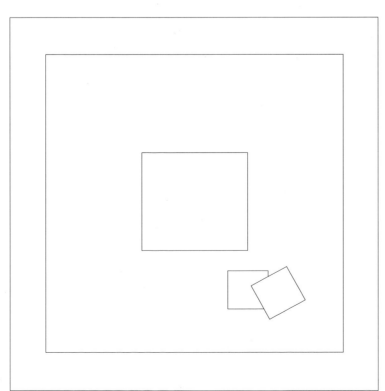

Use this pattern as a guideline for making this card with different papers and embellishments.

1 1 3

Love Blossoms

Here is a fun card for a birthday or graduation. Inside this file folder, you can add a card with as many pages, or "files" as you like. Why not create one for each year? If you have all twelve years of school pictures in order, this can make for a great memento! You can even glue on a button and a bit of seam binding to keep it closed. These little file folder cards come in several sizes and from a few different companies.

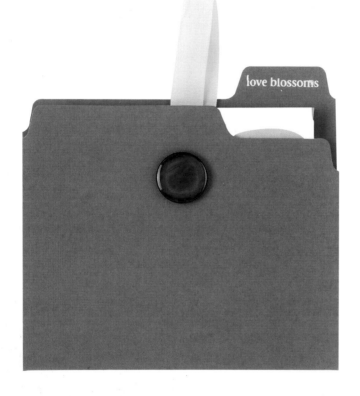

Materials

card: rose file folder

4¼" × 12" (11cm × 30cm) polka dot paper

three small photos or color copies

rub-on words

10" (25cm) piece of ½" (2cm) wide yellow seam binding

decorative button

white gel pen

Diamond Glaze

double-sided tape

craft knife or scissors

eyelet setter or tweezers

ruler

Resources

rose file folder by FoofaLa • polka dot paper by Frances Meyer • rub-on letters by Making Memories (Simply Stated collection)

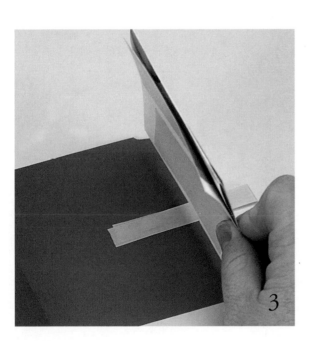

1 **Score and Fold Paper** Place the polka dot paper decorative-side up and in the horizontal position. Measure over 4" (10cm) and 8" (20cm) from the left edge and score vertically. (For instructions, see page 14.) Fold the left panel forward and the right panel back. Trim the sides so that they are even. It is always better to trim your paper after it is folded to ensure that the edges line up properly.

2 **Add Photos and Words** Lay the paper flat and adhere one photo to each of the panels with double-sided tape. Place the rub-on words on the paper and rub them with your eyelet setter or the blunt end of your tweezers to transfer. Refold the paper as you did in step 1.

3 **Add Seam Binding and Paper** Cut a 6" (15cm) piece of seam binding and fold it in half to make a loop. Adhere the loop to the inside right panel of the file folder card, allowing it to stick out about ½" (1cm). Position the left edge of the polka dot paper against the inside fold of the file folder card. Adhere the back of the first panel of paper to the inside right panel of the card with double-sided tape.

4 **Mark Button Placement** Close the card and fold the seam binding loop around the front. Use your gel pen to mark a small dot at the end of the seam binding to indicate the button placement.

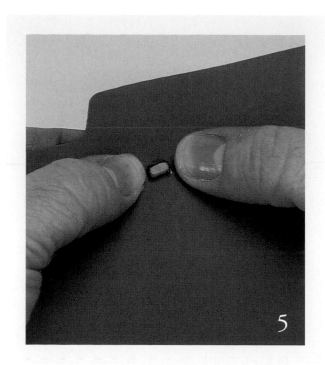

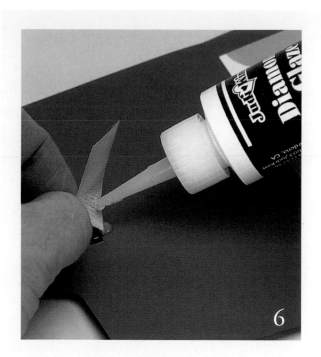

5 **Add Button to Card** Open the card and cut a tiny slit at the mark with a craft knife. Push the button shank through the slit.

6 **Adhere Button** To finish the card, thread the remaining seam binding through the button shank, trim the ends at an angle and glue them to the inside left panel of the card with a small amount of Diamond Glaze.

Use this pattern as a guideline for making this card with different papers and embellishments.

Cherished Friendship

These little file folders make such fun fold-out cards. Jazz up the outside with stickers and scraps of printed paper.

file folder	FoofaLa
papers	Making Memories
quote stack	DieCuts with a View
eyelet	Coffee Break Design
stickers	K&Company

On the inside, continue using the same paper. Layer it with a photo and a quote printed on vellum. Attach with double-sided tape, or let your Xyron machine do the sticky work for you.

What is Beauty?

This project is a no-brainer for those who love buttons and bows. Pearl mica gel is a wonderful gel medium infused with mica flakes. You spread it on with a paintbrush, and it dries to a soft, sparkly finish. The gel is also strong enough to secure small buttons. All you need is a bit of perky paper, some fancy buttons and seam binding, and you're on your way to making a beautiful keepsake card.

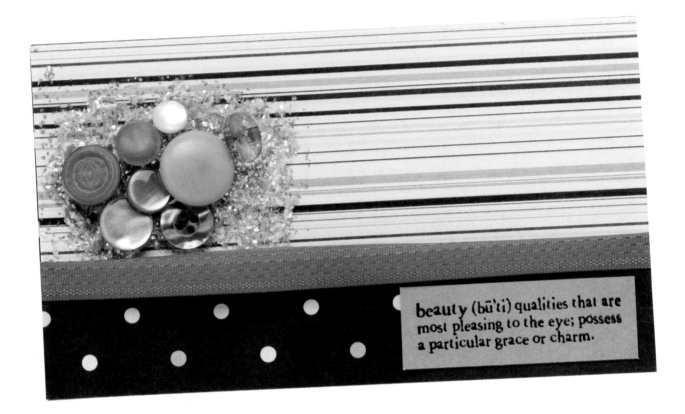

Materials

card: 6" × 6" (15cm × 15cm) striped cardstock

3½" × 6" (9cm × 15cm) brown polka dot cardstock

1¼" × 2½" (3cm × 6cm) scrap of pink cardstock

"beauty" rubber stamp

assorted buttons

16" (40cm) piece of ⅛" (0.3cm) wide pink seam binding

pearl mica flake gel medium

black permanent ink

paintbrush

double-sided tape

craft knife or scissors

ruler

cutting mat

Resources

cardstock by Making Memories • rubber stamp by Postmodern Design • gel medium by Golden • black permanent ink by StazOn

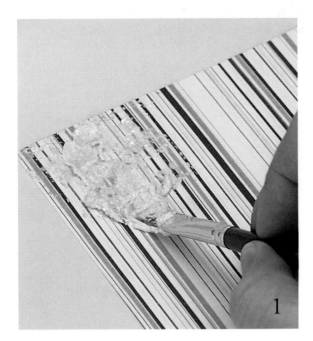

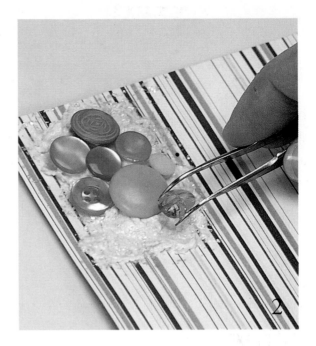

1 **Apply Gel Medium** Position the striped cardstock horizontally on your work surface and paint a very thick layer of gel medium on the top left corner.

2 **Embed Buttons** Embed several buttons of various colors and sizes into the gel medium. Set aside to dry for at least two hours.

3 **Score Cardstock** Position the dry cardstock so that the gel medium is in the bottom right corner. Measure over 3½" (9cm) from the left edge and score vertically. (For instructions, see page 14.) Fold and crease.

4 **Adhere Polka Dot Cardstock** Apply double-sided tape to the entire inside left panel of the cardstock and position the left edge of the brown polka dot cardstock against the inside fold. Close the card and press down to adhere.

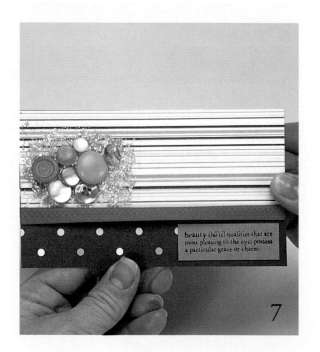

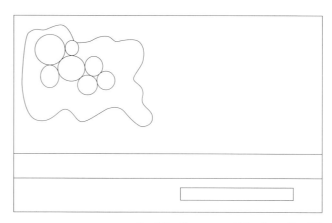

Use this pattern as a guideline for making this card with different papers and embellishments.

5 **Stamp Message onto Cardstock** Ink the rubber stamp with black permanent ink and stamp it onto the pink cardstock. Trim to approximately ½" x 2¼" (1cm x 6cm).

6 **Adhere Stamped Message** Position the card so that the fold is at the top. Adhere the stamped cardstock to the bottom right corner of the card with double-sided tape.

7 **Add Seam Binding** To finish, fold the seam binding in half lengthwise and wrap it around the front of the card, approximately 1" (3cm) from the bottom. Adhere with Diamond Glaze. Tie the seam binding into a bow on the inside of the card and trim away excess.

Legacy

In this card, I used metallic mica chips and glitter to accent some beautiful antique buttons and a metal sticker. Depending on how heavy your buttons are, you may need extra postage to send this card.

papers	Bazzill Basics Paper
	K&Company
sticker	Li'l Davis Designs

Don't Worry, Be Happy

Not all antiques are dark, as you see with the colorful antique buttons I used here! I also added sequins and crystal beads, which can be positioned into mica gel easily.

| papers | DieCuts with a View |
| glitter | Golden |

Belt to Last

Remember the first belt you made in Home Economics? Okay, if you are too young to have had Home Ec in high school, I'll give you a quick lesson in this project. This is a great idea for your next scrapbook album or altered book, since the belt can be tightened to fit bulging pages.

Materials

7" × 7" (18cm × 18cm) white cardstock folded to 7" x 3½" (18cm × 9cm)

4¼" x 7" (11cm × 18cm) kiwi cardstock

acetate with leaf pattern

11" × ½"(28cm × 1cm) strip of plaid fabric

two silver belt loops

rusty star

decorative stamp

celery dye ink

Diamond Glaze

double-sided tape

craft knife or scissors

eyelet setter or tweezers

ruler

cutting mat

Resources

white and kiwi cardstock by Memory Box • acetate by Magic Scraps (Serenity collection) • rusty star by Pedlar's • belt loops and nickel rectangles by 7gypsies • decorative stamp by JudiKins (Rough Age collection) • dye ink by Marvy

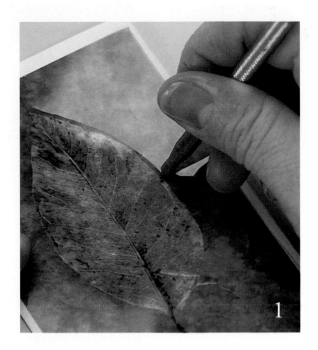

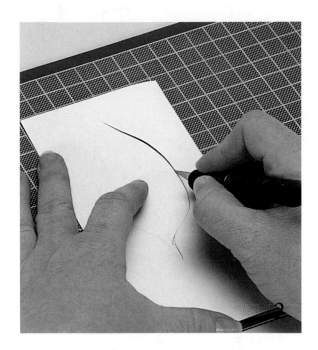

1 **Prepare Card with Acetate** Trim the acetate to 7" × 3½" (18cm × 9cm), centered around the leaf. Place the acetate on the front of the white card and trace around the leaf with your eyelet setter or the blunt end of your tweezers to transfer the shape onto the card.

2 **Cut Out Leaf Shape** Use a craft knife to cut out the leaf shape through the front and back panels of the card.

3 **Position and Adhere Acetate** Position the acetate inside the card, lining the leaf up with the cut-out windows. Adhere the acetate to the inside front flap of the card with double-sided tape, then apply more tape to the inside of the card around the acetate. Close the card and press to adhere.

4 **Stamp Image** Apply celery dye ink to the decorative stamp and stamp the image randomly onto the top three-fourths of the card on both sides. Set the card aside to dry.

1 2 3

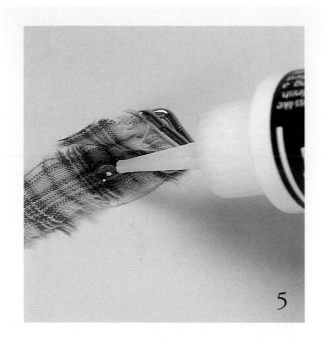

5 **Add Belt Loops to Fabric** Place the fabric horizontally on your work surface and pull the threads on the sides to fray the edges. Position two belt loops on the fabric, approximately ½" (1cm) from one end. Pull the fabric through both belt loops, fold it over and secure it in place with Diamond Glaze.

6 **Adhere Rusty Star** Use Diamond Glaze to glue the rusty star onto the fabric near the belt loops, as shown. Set the fabric belt aside to dry for at least ten minutes.

7 **Add Belt to Panel** When the fabric belt has dried, wrap it around the leaf card from step 4 to divide the stamped and unstamped areas. Fasten the belt, secure it to the card with Diamond Glaze and trim off any excess fabric.

8 **Add Panel to Card** To finish, place the kiwi cardstock face down on your work surface. Measure over ¾" (2cm) from the left edge, score vertically, fold and crease. (For instructions, see page 14.) Apply double-sided tape to the narrow panel of the kiwi cardstock. Position the open side of the leaf card against the fold in the kiwi cardstock and close the flap. Press to adhere.

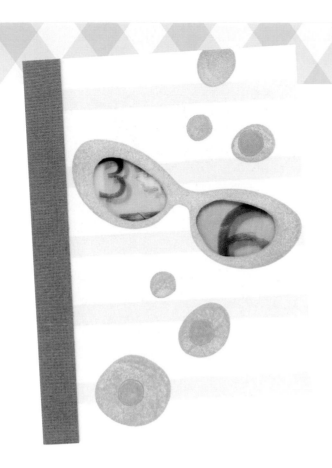

Made in the Shade

This card may not be all buttons and bows, but it sure does scream "accessorize!" Stamp a cool image onto decorative paper, use a craft knife to cut out the inside shapes, and then add fabric, acetate or photos.

papers	Bazzill Basics Paper
stamp	JudiKins
acetate	Magic Scraps

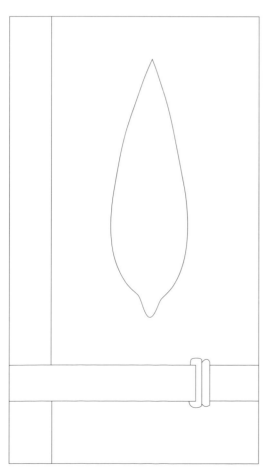

Use this pattern as a guideline for making this card with different papers and embellishments.

RESOURCES

American Art Stamp
310-371-6593
www.americanartstamp.com

Amy's Magic Leaf
724-845-1748

Anna Griffin
1-800-817-8170
www.annagriffin.com

Apropos
509-624-1754
www.aproposartstamps.com

ARTchix Studio
250-370-9985
www.artchixstudio.com

Autumn Leaves
1-800-588-6707
www.autumnleaves.com

Bazzill Basics Paper
480-558-8557
Fax: 480-558-8558
www.BazzillBasics.com

Carolee's Creations
435-563-1100
www.caroleescreations.com

Clipiola
1-800-226-5287
www.cavallini.com

Coffee Break Designs
703-250-6684

EK Success
www.eksuccess.com

Emagination Crafts
1-866-238-9770
www.emaginationcrafts.com

FoofaLa
402-330-3208
www.foofala.com

Golden Paints
607-847-6154
www.goldenpaints.com

Hanko Designs
510-523-5603
www.hankodesigns.com

Heidi Grace Designs
1-866-89-HEIDI
www.heidigrace.com

Hero Arts
1-800-822-4376
www.heroarts.com

JudiKins
310-515-1115
www.judikins.com

K&Company
1-888-244-2083
www.kandcompany.com

Li'l Davis Designs
949-838-0344
www.lildavisdesigns.com

Making Memories
1-800-286-5263
www.makingmemories.com

MaryJo McGraw
www.maryjomcgraw.com

Marvy Uchida
1-800-541-5877
www.uchida.com

Memory Box
1-888-723-1484
www.memoryboxco.com

Mrs. Grossman's
1-800-429-4549
www.mrsgrossmans.com

Pebbles, Inc.
801-235-1520
www.pebblesinc.com

Postscript Studio/ Carmen's Veranda
714-528-4529
www.postscriptstudio.com

Postmodern Design
405-321-3176

Pressed Petals
1-800-748-4656
www.pressedpetals.com

Savvy Stamps
360-833-4555
www.savvystamps.com

Scrappin' Dreams
417-831-1882
www.scrappindreams.com

Stampendous!
1-800-869-0474
www.stampendous.com

Xyron
1-800-793-3523
www.xyron.com

INDEX

 # Look for these other great North Light Books by MaryJo McGraw!

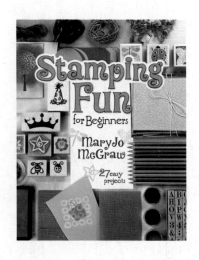

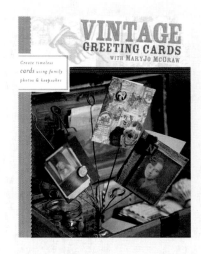

Stamping Fun for Beginners

ISBN 1-58180-585-3, paperback, 112 pages, #33054-K [2004]

This user-friendly handbook is indispensable for newcomers to stamping, as well as a great quick-reference guide for seasoned artists. It's full of easy-to-follow instructions on dozens of techniques, as well as 27 easy projects from greeting cards and gift tags to boxes, jewelry, journals and more. This book is a must-have for anyone who is into stamping and having fun!

Vintage Greeting Cards with MaryJo McGraw

ISBN 1-58180-413-X, paperback, 128 pages, #32583-K [2003]

Vintage, nostalgic and retro chic themes are the hottest trends in crafting, and now you can add these looks to your handmade greeting cards. This book features keepsake card projects using family photographs, paper ephemera, vintage trinkets and retro styling. Twenty-three step-by-step projects and tips throughout the book make it perfect for beginning or advanced cardmakers.

Greeting Cards for Every Occasion

ISBN 1-58180-410-5, paperback, 128 pages, #32580-K [2004]

Create heartwarming, handcrafted cards for every occasion! You'll find basic techniques, tips and guidance for crafting personalized greeting cards for your family and friends. Each project features clear, step-by-step instructions using stamps, decorative paper and other easy-to-find materials. Plus, you'll discover MaryJo's gallery of ideas for making cards to celebrate the special events in your life.